M000222905

This book is dedicated to the community of single ladies navigating through singlehood, trying to figure it all out. Hopefully this book will make you laugh, but more importantly I pray it will make you think twice before giving your most precious gift as a single woman—monogamy, and all of the gifts that come with it—to a man who has not shown himself to be deserving of it. And to my mom, who was married five times and wanted more than anything to prove to me that love works. R.I.P. Mommie.

DATE, *Girl!*

*143 Reasons Why I Believe Women Should
Date Multiple Men*

Stacii Jae Johnson

Copyright 2015 by Stacii Jae Johnson. All rights reserved. This material is general dating advice only and is not intended to be a substitute for professional, medical, or psychological advice or counseling. This book, or parts thereof, may not be reproduced in any form without permission from the publisher; exceptions are made for brief excerpts used in published reviews. For permission requests, write to the publisher, addressed "Request Permission Coordinator," at the website below.

Stacii Jae Johnson
www.staciijaejohnson.com

Published by
Waterhouse Publishing
270 17th Street, Unit 708 Atlanta GA 30363

Date, Girl 143 Reasons Why I Believe A Woman Should Date Multiple Men/ Stacii Jae Johnson --- 1st Ed.
ISBN- 10: 0-692-54450-X
ISBN -13: 978-0-692-54450-1
Title ID: Date, Girl

Printed in the United States.

This book is available for individual and quantity discounts given for bulk purchases. Contact@StaciiJaeJohnson.Com

For information on bringing Stacii Jae Johnson to your live event or to book an event, email: BookStaciiJae@staciijaejohnson.com

Website: Www.StaciiJaeJohnson.Com
Website: Www.TheSingleGirlsClub.Com

Note to Self as a Single Girl

Never Forget Me!
Never Forget My Happy!
I Will Never Forget
Living, Loving, Laughing, Learning ME!
All of Me
I Am the Fullness of Me Operating From the ONE—Me
Single and Fierce
Proud of Me
Now
Using For My Testimony Who I Used To Be—Me No More
Naw, That Ain't Me
Depressed Me
Mad Me
Hurt Me
Going on Dates to Find My Happy
But Still Sad
Not Being Me
Depressed
Mad
Being You and What Your Vision of Me Is
No More!
No More!
No More!
Now
I am Living, Laughing, Learning, Loving Me!
And the Best Part Is, I Asked Me
What Makes ME Happy And
It's......

—Stacii Jae Johnson

I love to see a young girl go out and grab the world by the lapels. Life's a bitch. You've got to go out and kick ass.

— Maya Angelou

When you are going through something and you feel like your light isn't shining and you are in the fire, STAND in the fire and DARE it to burn you.

— Stacii Jae Johnson

Table of Contents

Acknowledgements

There are so many people who have been instrumental in my growth. I have to start with my mommie. You always encouraged me to reach for the stars. Anything I put my mind to accomplish, you said I could. I have carried that with me all of my life. I believe that is what gives me my audacious spirit. Not a day goes by that I do not think of you. My life has been forever changed since you have been gone. You are my angel in heaven.

My grandmother for always giving me the truth, everything I needed to hear; raw and sometimes hard to bear, but definitely necessary. My sister Crystal for loving me unconditionally.

My guidance counselor Mrs. Logan who guided me when I was a high school student, and honestly made sure I didn't veer so far off course being "Ms. Popular" that I did not do the things that mattered. With your help, not only did I get accepted to Spelman College, I was accepted to all five colleges to which I applied.

Dr. Glenda Dickerson, my college drama professor, rest in peace, thank you for the prophecy my junior year at Spelman College. As a young drama student with my eyes on becoming a famous actress with all the bells and whistles, I hated what you said, but you were so right on. My life has been a creative journey, but I have always had a business backdrop, a plan, and a strategy pushing it forward. You were right—I was destined to do much more than be an actress.

Freddye Hill, the Dean of Academics at Spelman College. You allowed me back into Spelman after not withdrawing properly and twirling off when I got accepted to The American Academy of Dramatic Arts in Los Angeles. If it were not for you and your belief in me, I would not have been admitted back into Spelman a year after leaving and been able to graduate with my Cum Laude Bachelor of Arts degree.

Jamie Foster Brown, my mommie #2. Thank you for being you. Having you in my life has been a breath of fresh air. God called my mom at age 56 and then gave me you. You are a prayer answered.

Shanti Das, Taurea Avant, Nicole LaBeach, all published authors, you three are my "can do" motivation. Looking at your success, because I had touched you all and watched your journey, writing a book seemed doable. It was encouraging to have people in my life that had accomplished becoming an author. Shanti, thank you for motivating me from the beginning. Taurea, thank you for the hands-on direction and for pushing me to "just get it done."

Charles Johnson, thank you. Without you I never would have started on this single girls journey. Learning D.I.C.E. (dependable, inspiring, complementary, enhancing) changed my life. I never really knew what I needed a man to be in my life, before you introduced D.I.C.E. to me.

Giovanni DiPalma, my big brother, who was there to help me out of a situation when no one else would. It's like they say, you never know who the person will be to get you out of a tight spot. That's why I try to do good by everybody. Your support is much appreciated.

Kasim Reed, Mayor of Atlanta, thank you. To work on your leadership team as the Director of Entertainment & Special Events for the City of Atlanta was laced with many life changing experiences. Through all of them, no matter what they were, I became a better me. You gave me the space as the leadership in that office to spearhead what we both knew had the potential to become the multi billion dollar film industry it is now in Atlanta. It feels like yesterday that I came into your office and told you that the city was only getting $50 for film street closures. As a leader and CEO of the city, you believed in me, saw the vision, supported my ability to lead the vision, and now, looking it all, WOW!

Shout out to all of my favorite ladies in Office of Mayor Reed who do the heavy lifting that keeps the city moving forward: Candace, Cathy and Katrina; Joy, DiDi and Deshanna, having you on my team while at the city, was a joy. You all were the BEST!

Reggie Rouse, CBS Radio, WVEE V-103 Program Director, thank you for recruiting me to be one of your live on-air jocks at the #1 urban radio station in the country. After only being in radio for 15 months on WAEC, Love 860 AM, with my Black Girls Radio show, you brought me over to the big leagues. Working with the BEST radio team in the country was a dream come true.

Thank you to the media and business superstars, who are leaders in their respective industries, and who have supported me professionally over the years in the growth of the Stacii Jae Johnson brand: Angela (10SquaredPR), Saptosa (135th Street Agency), Jessica (Campbell Manning PR), Quisa (F2 Communications), Nick and Tirrell (Go Liquid Soul), Yvette Caslin (Steed Media Group), Henry (Southern Hospitality Transportation) and Christian (One Stop Productions), Jay (VOD Photos), Sean Cokes (The Artistry Group), Quintavious (QJS Design Studios), Derek J (The J. Spot Salon) and Ericka Dotson (Indique Hair). Thank you #teamstaciijae: Christian aka @geishaboi (Makeup), Pennae of Salon Pennae (Hair) and Lord Brody (Stylist) for being the best glam team a girl could ask for. Shawn Bell (Media Doctor Services), thank you for creating the best d*mn website I ever had, and Terrence Crowley, your videos ROCK! Thank you also to my extra-smart attorneys Jerry Caldwell and Donald Woodard, and to my amazing spirit guides and life coaches who keep me grounded, Jennifer Lester and Sheri Riley. I love and appreciate #teamstaciijae more than you all will ever know.

Tangie, Mari, Sheila, Angel, Dwayne, Nicci, Zelda, Christine, Q, Rasheem, Mona, Evens, Marc, Tiffany, and Kasi, thank you all for your friendship. I know I am a LOT! And being friends with me is NOT easy. CJ and Simone for rocking with me and seeing my vision for Black Girls Radio (BGR). You were both an integral part of the BGR being the #1 girl talk radio show in Atlanta. Thank you, Bernard, for introducing me to Barkue, my manager. Barkue, I am so excited about what we are about to accomplish. You showed up right in the nick of time. A prayer answered.

Introduction

The problem: girl meets guy. She knows what she wants and has dated enough men to know what she likes. Girl likes guy, and there you have it—she is off the market and fully dedicated to him. After I decided that he was what I wanted, I totally took myself off the market. I became committed to just him. And that would have been fine, if at that point he had done the same. All of my girlfriends dated like that, so I didn't think twice about it. I never really considered going about dating any other way until about three years ago, when some things happened in my life to make me stop and look at who I was, both personally and professionally. As I began to work on myself, I had two relationships back to back, each lasting for about eight months, with about three months after each that I took to get myself together mentally after the break ups. So the total time, including the time I spent with the two guys, was just two months shy of two years. I asked myself, why didn't either of these relationships work? I always believe I am the cause and not the effect, so I did not want to victimize myself and ask what these guys had done to me, but rather, what had I done to myself? What was my role? What is my lesson?

In one of the relationships I found that I had typically made decisions out of fear that I would lose

1

him. I would think before saying or doing anything because I wanted to behave in a way that he liked. I wanted to dress the way he wanted me to dress, cook or even like the foods I thought he wanted me to like. I didn't want to be the stereotypical woman that always had something to say about everything, so I didn't really say much of anything. Plus, I was raised to believe that you have your girlfriends to really talk to about your life. That is what your BFFs are for. So with most of the men I dated I simply assumed the position, focused on him and didn't say much.

He was an attorney; very successful, and I was madly attracted to him. Most of our conversations were about him and his success and what he liked. I know that men like talking about themselves and about the things they want to talk about, so I did well by just staying in that box of discussion topics with him. I thought it was selfish and self-centered of him to never really engage me about my life; even if he did not really want to hear my answers, I felt he ought to have at least asked for the Cliff Notes version. But I dismissed his disinterest, as I always did, with, "That's just men." We dated for about eight months. I wanted it to work with him so badly that I found myself second guessing myself more and more. After looking at how I had been acting in relationships over the last ten years, I began to see that I had done this in many relationships. Why? Because I wanted them to work. Duh. I didn't want to do or say anything that was out of order that would cause the men to leave me. And the older I got, the less I said or shared about who I was, my wants or my needs. Because I needed them to marry me. Why? Because that is what my mom and all the rest of the world said I should want—Marriage. My clock was ticking. Thirty—the cut-off year—had come and gone and I was still single, childless and alone. Don't get me wrong, I could "get" a man. But I wanted the man I wanted. I wanted someone six feet or taller, educated, rich, with the wherewithal to build something and be wealthy. He needed to be fun, a traveler, have a pretty smile, be charismatic, a communicator, a provider, open minded to trying new things, spontaneous, spiritual, smart, and either have no kids or have kids older than 12, a man who wanted to travel, who had a passport open and was ready to see the world. Last but not least, he had to be willing to do anything to be my everything.

After many weeks of soul searching, I realized that the way I was going about dating was all wrong. In most of the relationships I had, I was choosing who I was going to give myself, my time and energy to way too early after meeting someone. Like I said earlier: meet guy, like guy, stop dating, seeking or making myself available to date anyone else. I know now that that was not the best thing to do. First of all, why give myself away to anyone without first *really* knowing who it is that I am giving myself away to? I didn't know the right questions to ask to really gauge who the other person was. Outside of the big stuff like infidelity, domestic abuse or straight-up lying, I was not sure of what qualities even to look for in a man that might indicate he was capable of delivering on the long list I had created, outside of what he shared with me verbally. And most times, what he said to me about himself was a lot different than who he really showed himself to me to be.

In their defense, I have to say that they were probably the men they were to me because I was the type of woman I was to them, which is not even 50% of who I really am. I would second guess myself on everything I would say, or text, or not say. I would try to interpret what everything they said meant. I would get headaches, I would be so confused and drained from the interaction. Being in a relationship was pressure; a lot of pressure that I now know that I put on myself for no reason. I felt like I had no control over anything. I felt like I was giving all of what he needed, bending over backwards to do any and everything, and he would do none of what I needed. But I always stayed, months and sometimes even years longer than I should have, trying to do all I could to make him fall in love with me. Don't get me wrong; I traveled to Africa, was given lavish diamonds, nice designer bags and introduced to moms, dads, family and friends with some of the past guys I dated. And because of that I could not understand why none of them ultimately asked me to take that next step of partnership. Yes, we have all heard of people marrying for the wrong reasons, so yes they could have asked, but thank God they didn't, because as I look back I can see now that I would have been miserable or divorced by now had I married any of them. Because not until we got married would I have started to be who I really was, and they would have been like, "What the hell!" LOL. The marriage would have given me the security that I felt I needed to be *all* of Stacii, and *that* would not have been fair to him or me.

What I realized was that my "problem" that I described at the beginning of this introduction—which

I will boil down here as only dating one guy at a time—was not the best way to get me to the life partner I wanted. The biggest issue was that I had not been out on enough dates with different guys just having a great time to learn what I liked, let alone enough to make a choice to date just one guy. Everybody that I met and decided I liked, I ended up dating for long periods of time, so all I knew for sure was what I didn't like from all of the failed relationships. I committed to each of them without initially knowing enough about them. As time went by I stayed, because by then I had time invested; I adopted the mentality that it wasn't all that bad. I made a conscious decision to live with all of the things I did not like. Despite being unhappy and unfulfilled, I remained loyal. I would date one guy for six months, another guy for eight months, another guy for two years, another guy for two months . . . heck, I even dated a guy for four years!

I was concerned, though, about changing my approach, because there were so many negative stereotypes of women who date more than one guy at the same time. Men date more than one woman all the time. Men have multiple women in the same zip codes sometimes. They have relationships going on simultaneously whether they admit to it or not. Men have women in constant rotation. But for a woman to do the same is generally regarded as slutty, and it is always assumed that she is sleeping with all of the guys she's dating. Well, first of all, I am nobody's *slut*. I am not sleeping around with the multiple guys I date and there are lots of reasons for me making that choice. The first is that I am not the type of woman who is comfortable sleeping with more than one man at one time. The second is the risk of known STDs. The third is that all of the drama that is created daily from everyone spreading themselves amongst the masses is not a life that I am attracted to living.

Let me define what I believe dating is. Dating involves me getting to know someone by going out with them for dinner, drinks, dancing, socializing with friends; going to movies, museums, concerts, sporting events; taking long walks in the park, etc. It does *not* mean being intimate with anyone. Dating three men at one time means doing all of the above with them, but with absolutely, positively, *no* promise of any kind of intimacy. Now, if you disagree and would like to engage in sexual exploration with all of the guys you are dating, that is your decision. Just know that you making a choice that comes with very high risks in every direction possible.

Some people think that women that date multiple guys are attention whores and needy. I can be honest and say that I do enjoy attention from the opposite sex. I believe every woman enjoys getting dressed up and then getting compliments. I honestly believe we enjoy even more waking up, hopping in the shower, going to the local grocer "unfiltered," no makeup or anything, and getting a compliment that means even more. But dating multiple guys will not mean you like getting attention as a woman any more than you already do; it will mean that you will get more attention than you do now, and if you are a bit insecure about how you look and what you bring to the table, dating multiple men will boost your level of security about your physical appearance.

You can really see how your unique connection with one guy is going to play out if you are dating many guys. The underlying problem in my relationships was being invested too early. I would latch onto something when there was not even enough there to connect with or latch on to. We would date until something happened, stop dating, and then I would go out, meet and date another person. It was a vicious cycle. Each time I felt it was not even the right thing to do. But I believed that anything outside of dating one guy at a time was wrong; it was for "bad" girls, and being a "bad girl" would definitely not move me closer to finding my life partner.

Now I know that if I had been dating more frequently, and dating more guys, I would have had a comparison and known more quickly when a connection was genuine and when it was not; and been more secure with myself knowing there are other guys out there with whom I did have a connection, and who were a better match for me. Another common belief about a woman that is dating multiple men at the same time is that she is not ready for a commitment. Dating multiple men at the same time has nothing to do with me not wanting a committed relationship; on the contrary, it has actually helped me get closer to knowing what I really want. I thought initially that dating more than one guy would muddy the waters, get complicated, and make me feel guilty. What I discovered was that there were only two reasons why these things happened. The first was if for any reason I was not honest in letting the guys know that I was casually dating several others. Honestly, not all guys will go for a woman that says that she is dating multiple guys, and in the beginning I shied away from the issue. Well, that's when it got complicated—because I was not honest. So I committed myself to telling the truth regardless of how it might make the guy feel. Heck . . . it's my life; I have to live it for me. The second thing was if I dated more men than I could handle . . . LOL. Anything more than three is too many for me at one time. I am a busy girl. I have a lot going on, so if I was dating too many guys I would get confused about who I had shared certain things with or who I talked to about certain things. Shucks, I would even get confused as to what each had shared with me, birthdays etc. Before I settled on three being my magical number, I dated freely as many as I wanted to. I would be honest and let them know I was dating other people. All I can say is—not good. It was funny to some of them. One had a running joke. He would say, "Naw that wasn't me, that was that other dude you dating," and we would just laugh it off. So three is my limit. I stop at that, and what starts to happen is that for whatever reasons one may fall off and I meet someone else, or I may let go of one of the less desirable ones to make room for another. I thought I would feel guilty, but honestly, I feel more empowered on my dates than I have ever felt in my life. There is no pressure, no headaches and it feels amazing. I am having a blast. And, trust me, a man understands that if he does not ask you to date exclusively then you are dating other people. It's usually just we women who limit ourselves before he even actually says he wants anything exclusive.

I also thought people would think that my wanting to date multiple men was because I did not want to take a risk on dating just one. For me, dating multiple men was ultimately about wanting to really take the time to get to know the person and know through our interactions whether or not he deserved me taking a risk on him. As with any risk, whether it be business or personal, I want to go in with my eyes wide open, knowing what the red flags are, and clear about my boundaries. During the discovery time, if I learn of anything that is not conducive to a relationship that I want to engage in, then I can unemotionally but kindly cut my losses instead of continuing to move forward in the relationship, blindly ignoring the facts.

I am no longer trying to be *good* at being *good*. I am working on being good at being *me*. I say what I feel and I say what I think. I don't hold back. If something that I say makes waves, so be it. I will deal with it. I don't always go with the flow anymore. I know what makes me—Stacii Jae—happy, and I don't live to serve anyone's needs before my own but God's. I cherish me. And I know that the man, my partner and my promise will cherish me too. And any man that doesn't can kick rocks.

I am the Multidating Philosofixer—a title and definition that I have created myself. A lover of helping single women fix their dating life by coaching them and guiding their philosophy on how to successfully date multiple people simultaneously. The premise of the Multidating Philosofixer is to (1) get single women to stop concentrating on an expected "result;" (2) be open to the journey that each individual date takes them on; and (3) not hand over monogamy on a silver platter until you know the man is deserving of it.

I am living my life now—for me. I am dating and enjoying my single life to the fullest. I have established some really cool friendships with some of the guys I have dated. If I was Stacii Jae dating one guy, I probably would have dated each for six to eight months separately and then ended up not being friends with some of these guys at all. Instead, because I am very clear on who I am now—having more "ups" than "downs"—I am happier with who I am today than I have ever been. My mantra is living, laughing, learning, loving ME! And I have found that as long as I stay the course and continue to do that first, then all of life is good.

DATE, Girl!

*143 Reasons Why I Believe Women Should
Date Multiple Men*

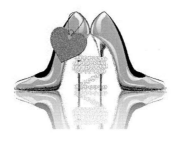

PART I: DISCOVER YOURELF

Reasons 1 – 17

1.
Most times we don't really know what we want.

Sometimes we believe we know what we want, but we actually want the wrong things. Take a look at that list of must-have qualities in a guy that you almost certainly have to have. How many of the things on that list are things that you think that you are supposed to want? How many are qualities that you were told by a mother, a grandmother or an auntie that a guy ought to have? How many are essentially superficial: your idea of physical perfection, or certain interests or hobbies that you think your perfect guy should have; things which, when it comes right down to it, may turn out to be much less important to you than things like, say, overall temperament? Ladies, we all start out here, but you don't have to stay here. Our perspectives are necessarily limited by our experiences. Dating multiple guys will help you to get beyond what you have previously believed was available to you. It will help clarify what you really want by giving you a solid idea of what is actually available. Your options are much more varied than you probably think they are.

2.

Use dating as a time to become more self-aware.

Are you dating someone that is good for who you are, or for who you wish you were or think that you intend to be? I am all for self-improvement—for self, not for a man—but at the end of the day, you're still going to be you, a person with a past that cannot be changed, and core values that make you who you are. Do you really understand how these things have shaped you? Dating multiple guys is a great way to learn more about who you really are, because it will give you lots of opportunity to watch yourself react to a lot of different things, and the key to self-awareness is self-observation. If you only date one guy at a time for six or twelve or twenty-four months at a time, you only ever see yourself reacting to one kind of guy and, more than likely, the same kinds of situations, over and over again. That's kind of like spending all of your time looking at a single slice of pie and believing you're seeing the whole thing. You're not going to get a 360° on yourself unless you see yourself from all different angles. Dating multiple men will give you that.

3.

You learn that you are enough.

Dating multiple guys will allow you to let go of desperation and insecurity about whether or not he is going to be "the one," a mindset that often tends to cause us to turn our scrutiny on ourselves as we worry about whether or not he likes us and whether or not we are going to scare him away by saying or doing the wrong thing. "F" the wrong thing. Be YOU! Dating multiple guys eases that fear a lot. While one particular quality of yourself might not appeal to one guy, another guy may totally love it. You gain a perspective that there is no single "right" or "wrong" when it comes to people; there are simply things that mesh together well and things that don't. You'll learn to stop tying your opinions of yourself to what some one man you are dating thinks about you, because it'll become impossible; you'll be experiencing too many perspectives on yourself. You'll begin to do what you do for you, and if you want to change something about yourself, it will be for you. In the meantime, you'll begin to realize that you are already enough just as you are, and you'll stop worrying so much about whether or not you are changing yourself, or can change yourself, in order to be everything to one individual guy.

4.

You get to really see how you are picking the same type of guys again and again.

This is a particular aspect of self-awareness. Dating multiple guys gives you an opportunity to really look closely not just at how you react to certain situations, but at what drives you into them in the first place. You begin to see the patterns in your life. Think about a color pattern of four squares—red-black-blue-green. If you only see four squares at a time, there's no way you can possibly see that it is a repeating pattern. But if you see twelve squares at a time, or a hundred and forty-four squares at a time, the pattern jumps right out at you. It's the same thing with dating. If you have three first dates in five years and each one turns into a relationship that lasts between a year and a year and a half, then you may miss the fact that in each instance, you were attracted to the guy because he initially showered you with attention and compliments that pulled you out of the funk you were still in from your last breakup, and that each one of these guys tended to have a manipulating, salesman-like personality that later turned into a major problem. If you have half a dozen third dates in a month, this behavior is going to jump out at you, and hopefully have you asking why, and will set you off on some soul-searching to figure it out.

5.

You ask yourself for the first time, "Does he make me happy?"

Say you find a guy that has every quality on your must-have list, and he loves you—does that automatically mean that he makes you happy? Say you go out with a guy in whom some of your must-have qualities are conspicuously absent, but you keep accepting dates with him because being with him is, well, fun. Can you be happy without all of your must-haves? Dating one guy at a time is like putting all of your eggs—your need for companionship, your desire to have fun, the pleasure of receiving compliments, the satisfaction of feeling attractive—into the proverbial basket. You're not likely to skip, or run, or take a detour while you're carrying your one basket; once all your eggs are in there, you'll do anything you can not to drop that basket and break all those eggs, because if you do, you'll have nothing. Think of dating multiple guys as being like having multiple baskets, each one containing slightly different eggs. You know if you break an egg or two, there's more where they came from—in another basket. Have fun! Juggle those damn baskets if you want to, girl!

6.

You will grow.

Dating multiple guys will help you learn new skills. You'll learn to handle rejection gracefully. You'll even learn to dish out rejection gracefully. Even more importantly, you'll learn that your self-worth isn't tied to anyone's rejection. You'll also take the opportunity to give a chance to a totally different kind of guy or pursue some little thing that interests you that you can't quite even currently name but that you haven't experienced before. You'll enjoy things that you would normally not enjoy or that you would overlook because you think it isn't enough, or because it isn't on your "list." Dating multiple guys will open you up to new things and cause you to grow. In this way, as you are dating multiple men simultaneously, you'll discover what it is in yourself that a guy appeals to and decide whether or not it's something that you want to continue to pursue developing.

7.

You get to know exactly what you don't want.

If you only date one guy at a time, you're more likely to compromise and put up with things that irritate you, make you uncomfortable, or basically turn you off because, well, you're in a relationship, and compromise, and putting up with each other's little idiosyncrasies, is what people in a relationship do, right? Um…maybe…but if you date more than one guy at a time, you have less invested in each one, and you don't have to put up with things that you don't want. You can pick and choose what kinds of personality quirks you are willing to tolerate, and yes we have to put up with some of those quirks and vice versa, of course. But dating multiple guys will definitely help give you clarity on which are absolute no-gos. You'll learn to recognize what you don't want sooner, and be more comfortable cutting it loose to make room for something better.

8.

It gets you out of your comfort zone.

We all like to be comfortable, no doubt. And to some extent we consider a date to be a good one when we feel comfortable with someone. But the discomfort of the unfamiliar can be very good for you. Being challenged—doing something new, being in unfamiliar surroundings, relating to a totally different kind of person than you are used to—can bring out the best in you. It can reveal things about yourself that you didn't know were there, and force you to be more creative. Getting out of your comfort zone by dating a guy that you might not normally date is a risk; but it is only by taking risks and getting out of your comfort zone that we can truly explore growth.

9.
You will learn who you are.

It has been said that we can only really see what kind of person we are in relation to other people; that is, who we are is revealed in our interactions. Who we are is not who we imagine ourselves to be when we're at home alone on the couch with a book and a glass of wine. Who we are is how we respond when a guy asks us to do something with him that we've never done before, like hike, or sky dive, or see an opera. It's what we do when we realize that a date is not going in a positive direction. It's how we respond to questions and it's the questions that we choose to ask. Dating multiple guys gives you tons of opportunity to interact not just with the guys you are dating but with the world in general, and through those interactions your personality and values will be revealed, not only to your dates, but to yourself.

10.

It's all about you and what makes you happy.

Dating multiple men will let you trade in all the drama of second-guessing yourself and wondering where everything is "going" for the possibility of having a good time right now, in this moment. You will have options about who you want to spend your time with, and what you want to do with that time. And the best thing is that this change doesn't just have immediate effects; putting the focus on what makes you happy *now* gives you a much better chance of being happy later, because you're much less likely to end up in a committed relationship with someone who doesn't really make you happy in the first place. And why waste your time with someone who doesn't actively want to make you happy? A guy that is not into you will make it seem like your requests are not warranted, and you will actually believe him. A guy that is really into you will go out of his way to show you that he's into you. A guy that really wants to keep you will put in an effort to keep you. A man that wants to be with you and only you will show you that it's all about you and your happiness. Let him show you what he's got.

11.

Bad habits no longer pull you into bad situations because you have options.

It's probably not news to you that we tend to keep ending up in the same relationship, with more or less the same person, and more or less the same problems, over and over again. It is extremely difficult to even see this pattern, let alone break it, if you are only dating one person at a time. But dating multiple men can bring the situation into sharp focus. Rather than gravitating towards the one man that is very much like the last one, spending time with different men, and different kinds of men, reduces the chances that you're going to end up right back where you were six months ago. For one thing, just making the commitment to yourself that you are going to date multiple men sets up a barrier between you and gravitating naturally towards that same wrong relationship. You may date the wrong man again, but you won't date him exclusively, and consequently you won't get sucked in so deeply. The problems that you have always encountered with a certain type of man—"your type"—who may not really be good for you, will stand out in sharp relief when you are also involved with men with whom you don't have those problems. Knowing you have someone else to spend time with will make it easier for you to let go of the bad situation because you have better ones to turn to.

12.

You ditch old and outdated belief systems and start coming up with your own belief system.

Your mama, grandmama, auntie and all the rest of the female elders in your family have their own ideas about what kind of man will make you happy. But who says they are right? You learn your first lessons about love when you are young and vulnerable and because of that you are not doing a whole lot of critical thinking. Nor do you have much experience of your own. Your mother teaches you how to be in a relationship as you observe the relationships that she has, including how she treats you. And as you start to get older and have boyfriends of your own, she probably dishes out advice from time to time. We soak it all in and believe it's the gospel truth, but is it? Well. . .yes and no. It's your mother's truth; formed as a consequence of her circumstances and choices, but it's not *your* truth—unless you choose to adopt and embrace it. Dating multiple men increases the chances that you are going to meet men who are completely unlike the men that you grew up around, men that come from, and can take you into, completely different worlds. Different men means different kinds of relationships; different worlds means different truths. As you continue to encounter new information and new ideas, you can continually shape and hone your beliefs about love; beliefs that are entirely your own, born of your experiences and choices; beliefs that fit you better.

13.

You feel more confident.

Being intimate with a man is an act of supreme vulnerability, and rejection in a serious and exclusive relationship that has been taken to that level can bring on a world of pain that can permanently strip us of some level of confidence. We often give the most of ourselves to men who aren't worthy to receive it, and suffer the consequences. Dating multiple men, however, changes that equation. For one thing, you are not being intimate with them, you're just dating them. You have less invested. Some of them will reject you. Some of them you will reject. So what? There are others coming along behind them, and because you have neither given too much of yourself or cut off your options, you don't stand to lose very much. Consequently, you aren't being stripped of confidence every time you decide a guy isn't the right guy for you. On the contrary, every time you make that determination, and do something about it, you are building confidence. You're getting stronger, smarter, and more desirable. You know your own worth, and it shows.

14.

You don't have to make a choice
to date one person unless you
truly know you are on the right
path with the right person.

Do you ever have a day where it seems like every man you look at is wearing a wedding ring, and everywhere you look you see couples? The pressure in our society to pair up is enormous, especially the older that we get. It's no wonder that we have a tendency to think of every date as an audition, and to hasten things along when it seems like we may have made a suitable match. But making the decision to date multiple men relieves that pressure. Dating multiple men allows you the time and freedom to enjoy the journey of each date. It gives you the time to figure out what you really want, and the time to figure out what a potential long-term partner really wants, without the angst that comes with exclusivity. And most importantly, you learn to live with uncertainty. Uncertainty is okay! You stop trying to figure out where every relationship is going to end up; the result becomes less important. Dating stops being goal oriented and becomes what it ought to be—fun!

15.

You will become less self-conscious.

There is an old adage that says that it's easier to find a job when you already have one. Why? Because there is less at stake. You already know where your next meal is coming from. You aren't desperate. You're not interviewing because you need a job, you're interviewing because you have a *career*. You're just looking for the position that you want; the right fit; the one you want to jump out of bed to get to every morning, for the organization that needs exactly the kind of talent that *you* bring to the table. Think of dating in this way. Similar to going on many interviews to find the right position, as you date you become more confident, more aware of your attributes, and more comfortable sharing them. You become less self-conscious and begin to really hone in on how the date is going. You are really present in the date. You learn to ask the questions that you really want answered, in order to discover if there is real chemistry, and if the guy is right for you. And if he's not, you simply move on, richer for having had the experience.

16.

You stop thinking that you will lose an opportunity to date someone if you say the wrong thing.

It probably seems like this reason is about having more options making you feel more secure, but really it's about allowing you to really be yourself. If you say what's on your mind, how can that be the "wrong thing?" Ladies, we have a tendency to cater to and accommodate men, even at the expense of our own personalities, and committing to one man too soon only exacerbates this problem. Why are you asking yourself whether or not you asked the wrong question or said the wrong thing, when you ought to be asking yourself whether or not you really like the man sitting in front of you? Why aren't you asking yourself if he is good enough for you, and how being with him makes you feel? Focusing all of your attention on how he is perceiving you is wasting your time. He's going to feel about you how he feels about you, and no single question or comment of yours on a date is going to change that. Focus on how you feel about him, and if you don't like him, move on. There's more where he came from.

17.

You may discover that superficial differences between men aren't as important as you thought they were.

Every girl wants to be with a fine man, right? And maybe you have rules about how tall a man has to be, or what income bracket he has to be in to date you. These things are important to you, and there's nothing wrong with having standards and preferences. But dating multiple men will reveal something to you that you might never fully realize otherwise: even if you only date men that have every superficial quality that you are sure that you want, you will discover that no two men are going to be the same, and the differences that are going to really leap out at you are going to be the ones that aren't so obvious. And it's those not-so-obvious differences between men that are going to be the ones that impact who you really decide that you like, and who you don't. Over time, it'll become easier for you to spot those deeper qualities that attract you to a man, and who knows, you may experience a shift in the superficial qualities that you may be attracted to. And as your ideas about what is attractive develop and grow, so do your options.

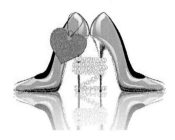

PART II: RELATE BETTER

Reasons 18 — 49

18.

When you meet the one that is an easy fit, you will know how to open up and receive what it is he has to give.

It is not easy to simply receive. Why? Because when we receive, we are vulnerable. The act of receiving means that we are open and available. Trust is difficult. So many times we remember the hurt from previous relationships. Giving, on the other hand, makes us feel in charge. When we give, we are in control. Think on all of the things that you do for a guy that you are dating exclusively, a guy that you like, whom you want to really like you. You probably give generously, like a fairy godmother waving the wand. Are you giving without any expectation of return, or are you giving because you want to crack him open so that you can actually get inside? You like that feeling because it makes you feel in control and powerful. Ironically, the ability to receive will come naturally to you when you date multiple men because you will know the man who is the "easy fit" when he shows up. You will enjoy receiving just as much as you enjoyed being an active giver—when you meet the one for whom you are enough, just as you are.

19.

You will know what a "Mr. Wrong" looks and smells like because the odor from him will be unbearable.

If you don't know what something looks like, then how do you know it when you see it? It can take weeks, or months for you to recognize and accept that a guy is essentially wrong for you, especially if he's the only one you are spending any time with. And often even when we do come to realize that we've committed ourselves to the wrong guy, by that point we're too invested in the relationship to simply let it go. But Mr. Wrong will be revealed to you much, much sooner when you see him in juxtaposition with guys who are better for you. And with the experience that comes from dating widely, you will be able to spot him immediately and avoid him.

20.

Even though he may not be the one, you may make a good friend.

Not every connection you make with a guy will be a romantic one, and chances are, most of them won't be. But one of the greatest things that will come out of dating multiple men is that you will make a very strong connection on a friendship level with one or two of them. You have tons of girlfriends that you love; why do you need male friends too? Plenty of reasons. Men like to fix things. Your girlfriends may let you cry your eyes out, and commiserate with you, but a guy is going to suggest something that you can do about what's bothering you. And guys understand guys. Who better to get insight into what's going on with someone that you're dating than to run his behavior by your brutally honest and not at all jealous (cuz he's been there, done that) male friend? Not to mention that a male friend who really gets you is much more likely to set you up with someone that you really hit it off with than, say, your grandmother is.

21.

He will respect your boundaries more.

Boundaries are a frequent issue in romantic relationships, but more often than not this is because we fail to establish them in the first place. In the beginning it is easy to get swept off of our feet and temporarily abandon everything else in our lives to be with the one person who has completely captivated our attention. Compound that, ladies, with our tendency to give our all to a relationship before it even officially is a relationship, and you have a recipe for disaster once the initial spell of attraction wears off. When you date multiple men, this issue rarely even surfaces. Provided that you are up front and honest about your situation and your intentions, he knows you have boundaries from the get-go. He also knows that he has no say in the matter because if he pressures or challenges you about it, he will simply be replaced.

22.

You stop concentrating on your list of 300 non-negotiable qualities that you must have in a man, and start being really open to what is in front of you.

There is nothing wrong with knowing what you want; in fact, knowing what you want, and what you need, and what makes you happy is key to finding a lasting and satisfying relationship. But that list of 300 qualities in a perfect man that you started making when you were six is probably not quite the recipe for happiness that you think it is. The reason for this is that no personal quality exists in isolation, and there are forces at work in genuine attraction that simply cannot be quantified or labeled. When you start dating widely, you not only discover that people can have desirable qualities that you never even dreamed that you wanted, you also find that some of the ones that you would have absolutely demanded actually don't make a damn bit of difference in the fact that you can hardly make it through one dinner with a guy. As you start dating multiple men, your list will both evolve, and become less and less important.

23.

The purpose of dating will
change from being about
finding the one to being about
really enjoying the one that is
in front of you.

It's almost impossible to talk about dating without
essentially talking about the search for true love, but
making the decision to date multiple men at the same
time is essentially the act of allowing there to be a
fundamental shift in your perspective. If you're not
concentrating all of your energy on whether or not he
likes you, and whether or not you are doing, or saying,
or wearing the right thing, then you free up a lot of
energy that you can use to think about other things, like
what you really feel like doing on a particular evening,
and which guy really makes you laugh, and how much
more you enjoy hiking than you thought you would.
The decision to date non-exclusively is a decision to
stop focusing on him and start focusing on yourself.
Rather than the purpose of a date being a stepping
stone towards a committed relationship or marriage,
the purpose of the date becomes the date itself. You
can't imagine how liberating this is, and how much
more fun you can have when your mind is actually on

what you are doing, instead of on where what you are doing is "going."

24.

You learn that relational values are as important as spiritual values.

You're a spiritual woman, looking for a spiritual man. What's wrong with that? Absolutely nothing, and by all means don't strike spirituality off of your list. But as you start dating a lot of different men who make the spirituality cut, you will start to realize that a sense of spirituality in a man, in and of itself, is no guarantee that he will be able to relate to you in a way that makes you happy. It is not an indication that he will be a good listener; or that he will open doors and pull out chairs for you; that he will encourage you to find the humor in any situation, or that he will always know just what to say to make you feel better on a bad day. Spirituality is no guarantee that the very tone of his voice will make you feel cherished and respected. Like every other quality on your list, it is simply one quality in a man which must function in alchemy with many, many others.

25.

When you are giving him what he needs, and he continuously does not give you what you need, then you feel more comfortable ending the relationship.

In a way, this is about the law of scarcity. The less you have, the more you seek to preserve. When you date one man exclusively, you're more likely to think in terms of negotiation and compromise, sacrifice and—well, let's be honest, settling—than you are if you are dating multiple men. When you take away the element of fear, it becomes much easier to make rational decisions about your relationship. When you are dating one man who seems to "get" you and treats you the way you want to be treated, it is much easier to see the one who doesn't, and it won't require a tremendous amount of will power for you to cut the one that doesn't loose. When you know that there are people out there who will treat you better, then the idea of continuing to see someone who doesn't becomes absurd. You'll gain the confidence you need to stop wasting your time with men who don't deserve you.

26.

You get to really see your own relational patterns.

A natural consequence of dating one man exclusively is that we tend to put a lot of emphasis on how the guy relates to us, and not so much on how we relate to them. That is, we see our own emotions and behavior as the unique and immediate consequences of something that is happening to us right now, when in fact, a large part of how we respond to others isn't about the others at all—it's about us. How we were raised, where we come from, the difficulties we have faced have all programmed us to perceive and react to things in a specific way, and all of this "wiring" is at work in every relationship that we have. The problem is that when we have one relationship at a time, over long periods of time, this aspect of ourselves is difficult, if not practically impossible, to see. Perspective is required in order to see patterns. Can you look back over twenty years and a handful of serious, long-term relationships and figure out your own relational patterns? Sure you can, but why would you want to waste twenty years figuring out something that you can learn about yourself over the course of a year or two by having an active dating life full of variety?

27.

You don't have to borrow your friend's car to do a drive-by.

Let's face it—scarcity breeds fear, and fear breeds insecurity. Say you're dating just one guy. The weekend comes up and he doesn't ask you out. Or you are calling and he won't pick up the phone. It crosses your mind to wonder why. Is there something else he'd rather do? Is he losing interest? Or is he just playing it cool? Or the worst—is he dating someone else while dating you? Once you start dating multiple men you will stop asking yourself these questions. You will no longer feel the compulsion to "just see" what's going on with him, because you'll be too busy with what you have going on. Plus, you will be about you, not about you and things working out with him. When you start dating multiple men, scarcity and fear go bye-bye, and then he'll be the one who will be doing the drive-by.

28.

You stop being the complaining, unappreciative, never-satisfied bitch on a date because you have more choices and you really don't give a rat's ass whether or not he is "the one."

He's late picking you up. He didn't make a reservation, and you had to wait in the bar area for forty-five minutes until the table is ready. You order a margarita and he amends your drink order, insisting that this restaurant makes a cocktail that "you absolutely have to try." You want what you want. You want your margarita. You push back—no to the cocktail that I "absolutely have to try." At which point he looks at you in surprise and then you see it flicker across his eyes: what a bitch! The worst of you comes out. You go on and on. You basically snap. You are disappointed. You had not been out on a date in at least four months, and this was your third date with him. You feel like he didn't think you were important enough to make plans to pick you up on time and plan a fabulous date, let alone even make a reservation. You expected for this date to be different than it has been so far. Blah, blah, blah. But honestly, it isn't really any of these circumstances that have brought out the worst in you, it's past disappointments; partly genuine, and partly brought on by assumptions and unrealistic expectations, and by your having put too much emphasis, and therefore, pressure, on how this date was going to go in the first place. You had your eyes on him to be *the one*. Realistically, though, there is no way to keep things from being less than perfect on a date. Shit happens and it's not always intentional. The traffic was bad. He's late. He didn't make a reservation, so what? If you're dating multiple men then you will be less invested in every date you have, which means you'll be able to truly relate to and respond to the person you are with, rather than them merely witnessing your relating and responding to your own assumptions and expectations. You brush your shoulders off easier and keep it moving!

29.

You have very limited expectations, so expectations are no longer the enemy.

When you are dating just one guy, expectations can quickly become your enemy. Why? Because usually you are grading a casual date on the "future hubby" scale rather than as just a date. Nothing is just what it is, in and of itself. Everything he does or says is an indication of how he feels about you and is a judgment on the type of man he is and you spend almost all of your time translating his responses. These expectations are not an inherent part of dating; but they are an inherent part of dating just *one* man. It can happen that we are disappointed so often that we try to abandon expectations altogether, which can lead us into accepting exclusive dating situations for which we should not settle. If you aren't fixated on whether or not he is "the one," then hubby expectations and conversation along those lines simply disappear, and are replaced by different expectations—that you will be treated decently, that you will have a good time—expectations that you should have on a casual date. Moment to moment. Nothing more. You learn that expectations, in and of themselves, are not an enemy.

30.

You will get to see the crazies more quickly, and when you do you actually leave, instead of making excuses.

I'm just going to come right out and say it—when you're only dating one guy, it can be hard to tell if he is nuts. Again, as I have said many times already, the root of the problem is investing too much in one guy too soon. The nature of investment is this: you give something because you expect to get something in return that is more than what you put in in the first place. To invest means to ante up and wait; any good investment advisor will tell you that only losers get scared by fluctuations in the market and cash it in too quickly. It's the ones that hang in there that get the real payoffs. So you rationalize. You make excuses, and you put up with things that you should not put up with because, well, you have invested in this, and you want your payoff. The key here is not to invest; at least, not to invest too much too soon. Dating multiple men will expose you to various forms of crazy, and you'll become adept at spotting each of them and moving on before you invest. And sometimes you will see the crazy is actually you. Investing too much too soon will sure make you crazy, because you will find yourself investing way more than what your return will be.

31.

You stop making assumptions.

One of the biggest assumptions you can make in dating is that you are both on the same page, which is to say, assuming that because *you* are dating exclusively, he is too. There are two problems with this. The first is that fear of not being on the same page can keep you from asking the questions that you really need answers to. The second is that putting all of your interest and energy into just one person drives you to make assumptions in the first place. Making the assumptions feels safer because it gives you hope. Even though it is a false hope, it is what you are used to. You are used to making the assumptions and not protecting your heart. If you are dating multiple men, the problem of assumptions largely goes away. You don't bother assuming that he's only seeing you, because you are seeing other people, and because of that you don't give a damn whether he is seeing other people or not. And that not giving a damn solves the other problem. Because you aren't so invested in the relationship, you aren't afraid to ask questions; you're also not afraid of the answers. You're not making decisions that leave you unprotected physically or mentally. And even if you care and are making assumptions about one man, you go on a date with another. After a while of being treated how you know you deserve to be treated by someone else, you learn that a man who really likes you shows it through his actions and his words and leaves no room for assumptions.

32.

You will learn to be honest, even if you are saying something that you think the other person doesn't want to hear.

You will find out very early on whether or not a guy can take who you really are, rather than the guy-pleasing version of yourself that you were always presenting when you only dated one guy at a time. The test for this is simple—you tell him by the third date you will be dating other people. If he can't handle that, then you're done, and you found out sooner rather than later. This is not a problem for you, because you are already seeing other people who don't have a problem with it—or you. Being honest also sets the tone for the relationship. He won't take you for granted, and you won't stand for it if he does.

33.

You get to stop being the "change a dude" agent.

We've all done this, right? You meet a guy that has some of the qualities that you're looking for, and some others that are, well, not so desirable. Rather than look at him squarely for what he actually is, we convince ourselves that the things we don't like are changeable, that being in a relationship will make him want to change, that we can turn him into all that we know he has the potential to be. If we're really desperate (and naive) we convince ourselves that love itself will change him, that he will want to do as much to conform to what we want as we are already doing to conform to what he wants. This kind of thinking is dead wrong. When you date multiple men, you get into the habit of assessing and accepting a guy for who he is. You can then take it or leave it.

34.

You will stop rushing things.

It is human nature to want to control how the story ends. That's fine, if you want to skip ahead to the last pages of an exciting book, or fast-forward to the closing scene of a movie because you just can't wait to see if the heroine is going to get her man. But life is not art. Life isn't about the end; life is about the journey. It's a process without output. When the right one comes along, the right things will happen that will inevitably result in a union. You do not have to rush anything. Dating multiple men will get your eyes off the finish line and onto the view. As an extra bonus, you can stop having to hear, "You're moving too fast, put the brakes on!" or "Let's just get to know each other" or "Why you tripping?" You're in no hurry to move beyond where you are, and why should you be, when you're having so much fun?

35.

He may not like it that you are dating other men, but it takes the pressure off of him.

Men don't like pressure, and not all pressure, like not all communication, is obvious and verbal. Dating just one guy almost unavoidably introduces expectations of exclusivity and, possibly, a serious relationship. Whether you ever ask the question outright or not, it's the proverbial elephant in the room. If it is in your head, and it's bothering you, then it's out there—in the energy you emit, in a look, in the tone of your voice. The only way to control the expectations is to not have them in the first place, and if you are happily dating multiple men, you won't. Knowing that you are dating other men, even if he doesn't like it, will take the pressure off of him.

36.

You'll stop compromising with guys who don't deserve the compromise.

We all know that compromise is an essential element of a good relationship. But continually doing what a dude wants to do because he doesn't seem to give a damn about what you want is not compromise. Neither is putting up with aspects of him that you really don't like in exchange for. . .what? There's a good chance also that you are not being fully who you are in fear that you may scare him away. So you compromise by being less than your 100%. True compromise can only happen between two people who are being completely honest and transparent with each other. Dating multiple men will free you of all the relationship traps—expectations, assumptions, insecurity—that cause you to compromise too soon, or for the wrong reasons.

37.

You get to establish a friendship.

One of the greatest things about dating multiple men is that you will make friends. An earlier reason talked about the advantages of ending up friends with guys with whom you didn't make a romantic connection. Even better is that dating multiple men gives you the opportunity to establish a foundation of friendship prior to becoming romantic—and intimate—with someone. If you spend a lot of time dating, you will discover things that you enjoy doing together. You'll find common values and build a history of common experiences. If your relationship with one of the men you're dating does evolve into a serious romantic relationship, then you will enjoy it all the more because you already know that you genuinely like this person underneath all of the sparks.

38.

You stop projecting what you want someone to be and start seeing them for who they really are.

Thinking that you can change or mold a guy is bad enough, but it's not as bad as not being able to see, or not believing what they tell you, they are in the first place. Say you spend five years dating one guy who initially told you he wasn't the marrying type. You're mad because you have no ring, there has been no mention of engagement. . .NOTHING. You're not happy, but you still stay for year six. . .This NEVER has to happen again. When you are dating multiple guys, you tend to believe them in the beginning when they tell you who they are, and you don't think or care to change them.

39.

You stop asking, "How do you feel about making us official?"

Making the decision to date multiple men doesn't mean that you don't ultimately want to get serious with the right guy one day, it just means that you haven't found the right guy yet. And until you do, you're going to embrace your singlehood, and enjoy it to the fullest. A lot of the pushing forward that we do when we are dating is because we are so afraid that something might not evolve into what we want. We are anxious, so we put the need and desire to make it official before every other consideration sooner rather than later. We want to prove to ourselves that the risk we took to just date one person, to spend the time needed to grow the relationship, was worth it. But if what you want is to really enjoy the opportunities that you have to build a strong unit, whether intimately or not, with the person you are with, then you no longer even feel the impulse to want to "make things official." Rather than projecting and pushing, you will actually start relating in the here and now and spend your time building a true friendship instead.

40.

You won't have your heart tied up in one guy anymore.

When you are completely invested in one guy, you stop seeing what else is out there. When you are dating multiple men, however, the exact opposite happens; you have a heightened awareness of your options, together with a sense that you deserve anything that you see that you want, and you have the freedom to pursue it—and I mean *anything* that you want, not just potential romantic opportunities. Rather than let the tone of your day be set by whether or not he calls, or where he wants to take you, your focus every day can be on you. What do you want? How do you want to spend your time? What makes your heart grow wide and open? What really makes you happy? When you're not allowing one guy to drag your heart around prematurely without having invested anything and according to his whims, you will have the time and freedom to ask yourself these questions, and to answer them.

41.

You will gain a realistic perspective about men.

This is particularly important since our earliest perspectives about romantic relationships are anything but realistic. As little girls, we think/believe/hope that all men are princes. As our awareness of our own surroundings expands, we begin to think that all men are like whatever our fathers, uncles, neighbors or older brothers are like—for better or for worse. When we grow up and get into a relationship, our idea of what a man is and can be changes and conforms to the man we are with, and over time, our ideas about our man become ideas about men in general that we carry with us. Women are prone to only date one man at a time, so theoretically, if a woman gets married early in her 20's or later in her 30's, and has mostly dated one guy at a time, she probably has little real perspective on men. Dating more than one guy changes this equation, because as you spend time with many different men, your opinion is constantly being shaped and honed by their differences. One guy may be an asshole, but another guy may be a good dude. You stop dismissing men with generalizations and start to actually see the man that is in front of you.

42.

You stop asking where things are going.

Part of the problem with serial monogamy is that you're always wondering where things are going. With one guy it's like you're following the North Star; it's all about direction. When you're dating multiple men, though, your life is a constellation. You never have to say again, "Do you like me?" You never have to ask if you are the kind of woman that he would like to marry, or if you are the marrying type. And you never have to say, "We are spending a lot of time together . . . I'm washing your clothes, I'm cooking you dinner . . . and you still don't seem like you wanna commit to me?" Pushing to find out where things are "going" pretty much means steering the relationship, and if you're steering then you're not relating. Relating means to feel sympathy with, to feel an affinity with, to understand. You cannot relate to another person when you perceive and interpret every interaction that you have with them through a filter of whether or not they are conforming to your agenda.

43.

You stop thinking that because he gave you a four-caret diamond ring and a heart-shaped diamond necklace that that means he wants to spend the rest of his life with you.

When you are dating just one guy, if there is even a little bit of anxiety or desperation, then you are liable to attach a value or a meaning to everything. There are three parts to any communication exchange. There's what someone means to communicate, there is what is actually said (or done) and there is how it is perceived. Unfortunately, because there can be such a vast difference in cultures, backgrounds, interests and expectations between people, there can sometimes be little to no relation between what someone means to communicate and what message is actually received. When you're dating multiple men, you get to stop driving yourself crazy wondering what that four-caret diamond ring "means." If you want to know what something means to him, you just ask. His answer is his answer. It doesn't matter to you one way or the other.

44.

There is no pressure to be a
person's everything. You just
show up and be present for
every date and make a
connection.

Somehow we seem to have "evolved" to the idea—if
you can call it progress—that we need to be everything
to our significant other. If we're dating just one guy in
the hopes that he will turn out to be "the one," then
we're probably trying to be his everything even before
making a commitment like marriage, kind of like we're
auditioning for a part. And auditioning is a lot of
pressure. You're putting it all out there for someone
who has the power to reject you, and who has no
obligation to tell you why when he does. This pressure
is all but non-existent when you are dating multiple
men, because you're not trying to get the part. Dating
multiple men is more like doing impromptu skits with
a friend just for the hell of it. Just for *fun*. Not all of your
skits will bring down the house, but from time to time,
without even trying, the two of you will cook up
something brilliant.

45.

You can be open and honest about who you are and what you want without fear of losing someone.

There is a temptation in dating, especially in the beginning, to put one's best foot forward. We don't set out to lie exactly; but we do occasionally omit certain pieces of information. We tell white lies. We may not exactly exaggerate the truth, but let's just say that we sometimes shape it in such a way that it presents us in the most flattering light. Why do we do this? Because we want the other person to like us as much as we (presumably) like them, especially when we are only dating one person at a time, and we only intend to date one person at a time. If they don't like us; if the first date doesn't lead to a second date, and the second date to a third, then we're left with nothing. And it's human nature to hedge against nothing. But if you're dating multiple people, then the concept of being left with nothing disappears, as does the fear that drives it in the first place.

46.

You are less likely to fall in love so quickly.

We fall in love too fast for a number of reasons. Sometimes we have an emptiness in our lives, or unfulfilled needs that are so painful that we seek to fill them with the first person that shows an interest in us. Sometimes we are essentially unhappy with ourselves, and we're looking to someone else to *make* us happy. Whatever the reason, falling in love too quickly can be dangerous. It can cause us to ignore red flags, and pursue a relationship that we ought to run away from. Making someone else the center of the world can distract us away from working on ourselves, or from making ourselves happy. If this goes on long enough, we can end up feeling as though we have forgotten who we even are outside of the context of a relationship. Dating multiple men will keep you too busy to fall into these traps. You won't spend every night at home alone. You will seek out the company of those who meet your various needs as you experience them. You'll have the confidence not to pursue unpromising relationships, and you'll keep the focus where it belongs—on YOU. In this way, when the time and the guy are right, you'll be ready for them both,

and you won't have to abandon your senses, or
yourself, to have them.

47.

You get a better perspective on
the individual guys that you are
dating, on what you like and
what you don't like.

Dating multiple men will help you to learn what
qualities you admire in other people. It will also help
you to define for yourself what you're willing to
compromise on and what you're not. And the more
guys that you date, the more quickly you will start to
see whether someone that you are going out with for
the first time is a good match for you. Having a better
perspective on what is in front of you will make it
easier for you to make decisions that are the best for
you. You'll learn to end things quickly and gracefully
if you are not clicking. You'll also learn to recognize
what you want when it presents itself.

48.

You learn that red flags mean run, and you actually run; you don't sit around for another decade, waiting for more red flags.

A common characteristic of women in an abusive relationship is that they stick around, despite having realized early on that things were not right. This is often because they have so much invested in the relationship—including their own self-respect for having ever initially judged him as being a worthwhile guy in the first place—that it gets harder and harder to walk away from a bad situation. Dating multiple men means you will *not* be so invested in any one situation that you can't easily walk away when you see warning signs; your deal breakers. You will be both free enough and empowered enough to let go of the situation because all that you'll be giving up on will be an acquaintance with whom it is not in your best interests to get any closer; not a boyfriend, or a potential husband, or your self-respect.

49.

It's easier to recognize the super awesome guy when he shows up; and the bullshit guy when he shows up.

The reason that it is often so hard to tell the super awesome guy from the bullshit guy isn't necessarily because we don't have enough experience with bullshit to recognize it when we see it. It's more that when there's only one guy in front of us, we want him to be the super awesome guy so much that we convince ourselves that he actually is. But if you're dating multiple men then it becomes much less important to you whether or not any individual guy is awesome. You enjoy the super awesome when he shows up, and when the bullshit guy shows up, you cut your losses and go your separate ways at the end of the evening. And the super duper awesome guy, if he is awesome enough, ends up being your one, two, and three.

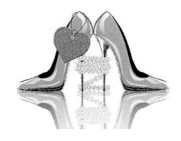

PART III: TAKE THE PRESSURE OFF

Reasons 50 − 61

50.

You have no expectations.

Expectations are difficult to control. In fact, in a one-on-one romantic relationship, it's almost impossible not to have expectations. Expectations are warranted and should be welcomed when you are in a committed relationship. But when you are only dating in the *hopes* of a committed relationship, expectations can sabotage us. Our expectations come from our childhood and adolescent ideas about romance. They come from our parents, and from the culture around us. Sometimes even when we think that we don't have expectations, they reveal themselves to us in disappointment and pain. But fortunately there is a cure for expectations: *exploration*. To explore means to go somewhere you have never been before, thus it is impossible to anticipate or predict what you may find there. Exploration is exciting! It is the place where you discover who you are at the core. It means to be open and willing to experience new things. Think of dating multiple men as exploration, and you'll never be sabotaged by having your own expectations too early again. You will also become connected to what the expectations you discover you have really mean to you, so if and when you are in your next relationship you will understand what is at the heart of what you expect.

51.

You don't have to worry about being everything he wants you to be and can just be you.

It's very easy, when you really like a guy, to find yourself going out of your way to accommodate him. Where you used to wear six-inch stilettos because they made you feel sexy and powerful, now you don't wear anything over two inches because he "doesn't like his women too tall." Where you used to do things just for you, now there's this little audience permanently seated in the back of your mind. When you do something on your own that you know he will approve of, like watch his favorite sports team on ESPN while you're home alone on a Sunday afternoon, or take a walk through a park that he has mentioned several times, you're not doing these things just because you want to; in fact, even as you're doing them, in your mind you're already rehearsing how you are going to tell him about it. No more. Dating multiple men makes this kind of behavior virtually impossible. Ever hear the saying, "You can please all of the people some of the time, and some of the people all of the time, but you can't please all of the people all of the time?" It applies here. So why try to please any of them by changing who you are? When you're dating multiple men you can simply be yourself, and let the chips fall where they may. For the right guy, you are everything he wants you to be just as you are.

52.

You're not sleeping with him, so you don't care who he's sleeping with.

Unless you are in a serious, committed monogamous relationship, the kind that is the result of an actual conversation between you and a guy, you should have no expectation that the guy you are dating isn't also dating, and perhaps even sleeping with, someone else. When you're only dating one guy, this type of behavior can be crazy and unacceptable, making the relationship very stressful. After all, you've already basically committed to him; why hasn't he committed to you? You know that he is not committed, but you continue seeing only him, hoping that one day he will be. Dating multiple men relieves this source of stress. You meet someone and start dating, but you make it very clear, right up front, that you have no intention at this point of taking the relationship anywhere sexual. Your intentions are to enjoy the date and get to know him—period. He may be sleeping with someone else, and you're cool with that. You don't worry and you definitely don't stress. If he wants to be with you and make it more than just dating casually, he has to prove to you that he's worth you making that choice. Eventually, if you both make it that far, that will include monogamy—dating only him. But until then, who cares? He can spread his wings and rest them wherever he likes.

53.

You can be completely honest.

I'm not just talking about "I'm dating other people" honest; I'm talking about be-yourself-and-let-it-all-hang-out honest. Wear the clothes you want to wear. If you don't like a certain kind of movie, say so. If you're not in the mood for Chinese food, tell him. Laugh when you think something is funny, and tell him if his topic of conversation offends you. When we decide that we are only going to date one man at a time, the first date can take on a strangely formal, best-behavior kind of feeling because we want to have a second and third date. You express yourself less, or if you do express yourself, you adjust a smidgen by being less honest with how you feel, so that he will go home wanting to see you again. From then on, it gets harder and harder to just be yourself. So you find yourself having less fun because you are being less of who you are. You rationalize that this is okay because he is still there with you even though you know you are not being completely honest. When you're dating multiple men, you have first dates all the time, and first dates stop feeling intimidating. You feel less like you are on a job interview or at an audition and you start to just loosen up and enjoy them. Maybe you don't get asked on a second date; but who cares, when there's another first date with someone else right around the corner?

54.

You no longer make decisions out of desperation.

You're in your late thirties. All of your friends are married or engaged. Your mother makes a point of telling you how much all of her friends are enjoying their grandchildren. You've been dating one guy for several years, and though he's decent and you feel comfortable with him, you have this nagging feeling that he's not "the one." But you have years invested in this relationship, and you want to start a family, so when he proposes you say yes, because, after all, this might be your only chance. You may not even be completely aware of all of these things, or articulate them to yourself, and at first everything is great. There's the excitement of planning the wedding, and within a year or two, maybe the excitement of expecting a baby. But there's going to come a day when there's no longer any excitement to distract you from the nagging feelings, and you're going to find that they never went away. It will be clear to you, then, that you made one of the biggest decisions of your life out of desperation. And girl, at that point breaking up your life and starting over again will be a hell of a lot harder than it would have been back before you said yes in the first place. Dating multiple men greatly reduces your chances of ending up in this situation. For one thing, you will have made an active choice, based on many, many options, about who you end up in the exclusive relationship with that eventually leads to a proposal in the first place. You will have many, many opportunities—and plenty of incentive—to tell "Mr. Almost" goodbye.

55.

Your main focus is no longer about where the relationship is "going." Who cares? You're dating several guys and having a good time.

Not all pressure in a dating relationship is pressure that you put on yourself. There is external pressure too. Your friends want to know how things are going. You've mentioned a guy to your mother a few times, and she wants to meet him. Months go buy, then a year, and people start asking you when they're going to see a ring on your finger. If you're dating more than one guy at a time, this pressure goes away. You are no longer communicating to anyone—consciously or unconsciously—that the one guy that you are dating is or even might be "the one" until he really is the one. Your friends and your family know that you're enjoying an active dating life, and if anyone does start down the when-are-you-going-to-settle-down road, you can quickly shut that conversation down by clearly articulating your current philosophy and leaving it at that. Their opinions won't feel so much to you like internal pressure when you don't share and agree with them.

56.

You stop judging your date in terms of what your children might look like.

Let's face it, if you're making the decision whether or not to go out with someone based on your chances of ending up with a short son, you're putting a hell of a lot of pressure on both yourself and your date. This is crazy. For one thing, it blinds you to all of the other great qualities that the guy could have, qualities that could make him look six inches taller in your eyes. For another thing, it shifts your focus away from the here and now, where you could be having a great time, and towards a hazy, imaginary, less than perfect future that will probably never happen anyway. When you are dating multiple men, you no longer see a first date as the gateway to marriage and motherhood; it's just a date. It's a couple of hours of conversation with someone whose company you think you might enjoy, and that's it.

57.

There's no more frustration about whether or not something is "working."

It's true that to some extent relationships either work or they don't; you click with someone or you don't. Sure, relationships take work, but that work is only meaningful, and worthwhile, if you're fundamentally compatible in the first place. But that's not the kind of "working" that I'm talking about here. What I'm talking about is the kind of "working" that has more to do with whether or not a relationship is proceeding at the (otherwise arbitrary) pace that you think it ought to. I'm talking about the pressure you put on yourself to hit milestones—one month, six months, a year; exclusivity, monogamy, spending the night together, going away for the weekend. . .An otherwise perfectly decent relationship can be damaged by the pressure you put on it to unfold in a certain way. When you're dating multiple men, this pressure goes away, because you're not focused on developing one single relationship in a certain amount of time, and the relationships you do have are not end-goal-oriented. Your focus is in the moment, not in the future.

58.

You have more time to do the
things that you want to do,
rather than always doing what
someone else wants to do.

You may wonder how this is supposed to work when
I'm telling you to date multiple men. When the dates
come less frequently you tend to change your plans
and possibly even start doing less of what you have
planned otherwise because there is an opportunity to
go out on a date. Most times when a guy knows your
attention is only on him he will probably be asking you
to do things with him that he wants to do. Which, if you
have both decided to be exclusive is, of course,
acceptable and more balanced than him always trying
to do what he thinks you want to do. But the point here
is that you're not in an exclusive relationship that will
make you feel pressure to compromise what you want
for the sake of his happiness. Sure guy number one will
ask you to do things that they're choosing, and he may
be in the habit of asking you to do those things last
minute and expect you to be available. But if you don't
want to accept, you don't, and you say so. And because

guy number two or guy number three is there, you know they might make you a better offer; an offer that is honestly up to the standards that you desire. So, you decline guy number one. And if he gets offended and doesn't call you again, who cares? You didn't want to do what he asked you to do. You were honest and that is all that matters. It is better to get to the end of the road with guy number one sooner rather than later.

59.

You are not so emotionally
attached after the first, second
or third date that you feel like
you can't see other guys.

You go out with a guy and you have a good time. You
make a connection, so you start thinking about him.
You go out a second, and then a third time, and you
like him even more. You enjoy each other's company so
much that it seems like going out with a different guy
at this point would be like cheating on him. This makes
no sense at all! For one thing, a connection is great; but
there are many different points to connect on, on many
different levels, and you have no idea whether your
connection with this guy will continue. In the
meantime, you might hit it off even better with
someone else—if you leave yourself the opportunity to
meet him. Making a commitment to yourself to date
multiple men will ensure that you don't pressure
yourself into a relationship with anyone prematurely.

60.

You're not as concerned about how your connection with one guy pans out.

Have you ever had a date where despite liking the guy, and finding him attractive enough, you just couldn't make a connection? Couldn't find any common ground at all? But not in a combative way; just in a mutually agreeable, "Wow, we really don't click at all" way? You both realize there is nothing there. No pressure. You keep it moving. But if you're only dating one guy at a time, there is a tendency to turn a small connection into a foundation that merits you committing. This is so premature. The connection may not be a firm road between you; it may be more like a tightrope stretched between two high-rise buildings where there is no foundation, only a mere connection. But you ride that small connection, make it more than what it really is and make a decision to date that one man anyway. If you're dating multiple men you won't worry yourself sick over how much weight that tightrope will hold.

61.

You have the time to really find
out who you are before
deciding to date just one person.

We've all heard heartwarming stories about high
school sweethearts who married at eighteen, grew
together, and celebrated fifty and sixty years or more
of marriage. It's a lovely story, but unfortunately, at
least in this day and age, it's of the fantasy genre. Half
a century ago people grew up more quickly. The world
was smaller, options were limited. Nowadays, it's very
common for women to have careers before thinking
about marriage and children, maybe even several
careers. Who we are, and who we can and are going to
be is no longer necessarily clear at eighteen, or twenty-
one, or twenty-five. Couple that with the fact that every
social relationship you have reveals more of you to
yourself. The average woman, by the age of thirty-five,
has only been in ten relationships that she has given
attention to for six, eight or nine months months, or
two, three or four years apeice. Men on the other hand,
by age thirty-five, have often dated freely and have had
many, many relationships which have allowed them

the opportunity to learn who they are before choosing the woman they ultimately want to be with. Dating multiple men and giving yourself a chance to fully grow into who you are going to be before deciding who you want to spend the rest of your life with more clearly reveals the opportunity for "forever" when you do decide to commit to one person.

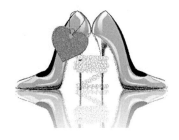

PART IV: GET EMPOWERED

Reasons 62 — 88

62.

It's much more fun than committing to dating one guy for nine months, and then starting all over with another.

Meeting someone new and being in the early stages of a relationship is exciting. There's so much to discover. Anything could happen. You want to do things together. You're comfortable together, but not so comfortable that you both don't still have an edge or a spark for each other. Not the kind of comfortable that ends you up wearing sweatpants every day and forgetting to brush your teeth. It's pure fun comfortable. Easy breezy. No more hard starts and not as many hard stops after only dating for a short time period. When you date multiple men, you get to live in a state of infinite possibility, and you can stay in it as long as you want to or don't want to. You date multiple guys until you connect with someone for whom your ideas of excitement and comfort and possibility shift naturally and mutually in the direction of each other. And until that happens of its own accord, you're having a great time. Think of it like an EKG; when you're dating multiple men you have a steady rhythm. You are confident to know that if the rhythm shifts it's a mutual shift in the right direction. Being in one failed relationship after another because you have decided to date one guy at a time is like living in defibrillation and having to continually get shocked back to life.

63.

You will stop second-guessing yourself.

When you are dating one man, and you're desperate for the relationship to go somewhere, there's a tendency to constantly second-guess yourself. Did you say the wrong thing? Did he know you were laughing with him and not at him? When you told him you didn't like fish, did that sound too bitchy? This kind of constant worrying saps our energy and robs us of both power and self-confidence. It is essentially giving our personal power to someone else, and letting them decide if we are worth their time and attention or not. Dating multiple men will let you stop second-guessing yourself because it changes your perspective from wanting them to approve of you to it being your role to approve of them (or not!).

64.

You can be in complete control.

There are several aspects to this, and they are all awesome. First, my philosophy of dating multiple men requires total honesty and transparency. If you're not trying to hide anything, then you are less susceptible to things getting out of your control, and nothing can get out of your control quite as quickly as a secret or a lie. Second, as I have mentioned before, you get to stop hiding parts of yourself, or shaping yourself into what you think he wants you to be, both actions that will put you in someone else's control. And last but not least, if you are honest, and he likes you, he'll start trying to please you, which puts you in the driver's seat for a change.

65.

You feel powerful times ten.

When I was only dating one guy at a time, I always felt a little bit like I was in the middle of a minor earthquake; nothing was falling down around me, but the ground beneath my feet just didn't feel steady. I have had some great relationships with some really great guys. But I always felt like they were all one foot in and out of the relationship. I stayed because I wanted them to work, and I hoped that as time pressed forward I would begin feeling like we were a team. I would feel powerless in those relationships, and frequently I lost who I was. No fault of theirs, though. But when I started dating multiple men simultaneously, I regained a solid footing to who I am, and reclaimed the freedom to continue becoming. I stopped caring whether or not either of those things fit in with someone else's agenda. I began to notice the absence of things that I had learned to live with for a long time—anxiety, fear and the prospect of loss. Now, when faced with the prospect of loss in one of my relationships, I still feel an underlying sense of being at peace because I no longer feel like someone who is leaving me is taking a piece of me with them. Dating more than one man at a time gives you a strong sense of yourself and will make you feel invincible.

66.

You don't take a fine piece of
real estate off the market just
because there is interest. Show
me proof of funds.

You have value! There are many men who will be
interested in you if they know you are available. But
just because a man expresses interest doesn't mean that
he's "the one." Before you hand over the keys, he
should be required to demonstrate that he is both
willing and able to meet the responsibility of a
relationship with you. If you have ever purchased real
estate, you will know that these transactions take time.
There are forms to sign. Disclosures. Inspections.
Dating is no different. Getting to know someone takes
time. And you don't get to know them only when
things are going well. In fact, you don't really know
them at all until you've seen how they act when faced
with trouble. The ability to observe a man over time is
your "proof of funds." Until then, you should still be
"on the market." The house ain't sold, until it's SOLD.

67.

Men love to win, and a man will
rise to the occasion if he knows
he is in competition.

Many women I talk to about dating multiple men are
not opposed to the concept, but they do get queasy at
the thought of telling a date that they are dating, and
will continue to date, other men. They worry that they
will offend him, or hurt his feelings, that he will
interpret their disclosure as not being interested in him,
or that he will think she is not a woman who is ready
for a commitment. Or that dating multiple men means
she is sleeping with multiple men, which I have
covered already and will reiterate now, is the furthest
thing from the truth. Dating multiple men and sleeping
with multiple men are two different things. This book
does not support the latter. Honestly, I have heard men
come up with the silliest reasons why they don't want
me to date other men while also dating them. I say silly
because they are usually very convinced that their
reason is substantial enough for me to declare that I
will stop—or else—and we all know what the "or else"
means. It's the ultimatum that we never want to hear
because as women we like choices. Well, I say don't
believe it. Do not believe a word of it. If he gives you

an ultimatum, then in your nicest, sweetest voice say, "I totally respect your decision. I am happy that we had this discussion. I would have wanted to not have our last date so soon, but I guess your decision leaves me no choice." Yeah, I know what you are saying. It is a strong stance to take. But you either stand for something or fall for anything. It's been my experience that no matter what he says at that table, it's much more likely that you're going to elevate your own value in his eyes. If dating you is a competition, that makes you the prize. Most men like competition. They enjoy winning. They will fight for what they feel is worthy and believe in. If he decides he does not want to be in the game, he honestly is letting you know what he feels you are worth to him. But if he decides to play, now he knows that he had better bring his best game. Game on!

68.

You will no longer have to throw yourself at his every whim.

The less interested that you are in a relationship, the more power you have. I am not against relationships, I'm only against premature and imaginary relationships! Boy meets girl, girl decides she likes boy, girl decides by the third or fourth date that she only has eyes for him. When you spend all of your time accommodating a man, you don't make your relationship stronger, you make yourself weaker. This doesn't happen when you're dating multiple men because it's about you and not them. When you date multiple men, what you decide to say yes to on your date, you do for yourself, and your own reasons. This makes you stronger. Throwing yourself prematurely at his every whim will no longer even occur to you.

69.

If you find out that he's not that into you, so what?! Who cares? There's lots more where he came from.

It's a fact of life that not everyone that you like is going to like you, and the converse is also true. That isn't going to change whether you date just one man at a time, or date multiple men. What will change is how you feel about it. It's all too easy to get your self-esteem tied up in what someone else thinks about you, or if you they think about you. Remember the piece of paper in grade school you had with the question "Do You Like Me? Check yes or no." And if they guy checked "no" it would be the worst. Well, first of all, I believe the girls should have never been the ones giving those notes to the boys. Getting a "no" definitely did not help my self-esteem. But when you're dating multiple men, your self-esteem comes from how you feel about yourself, as it should. Men will come and go, regardless. It's okay. The more that you meet, the better chances you have of meeting and knowing exactly who the right one is. If you're dating multiple men, then every relationship you have won't take a piece of you with it when it ends.

70.

You'll stop feeling like you suck at love.

Just because you're only dating one man does not mean that you're in love, or that he is in love with you now or that he will even love you later. Stop putting so much pressure on yourself, and get "the L word" out of your vocabulary. Thinking that you are bad at something only saps your personal power. Love is precious. Love happens over time. Love has to be tried. Discovering love is exciting. You don't suck at love. You suck at believing that you deserve to be exactly who you are and still attract the love you want. You suck at believing you deserve the love you want. So you meet a man that gives you a little bit of what you want and then you decide he is the one. Dating multiple men will get this nagging and unpleasant thought that you suck at love out of your head. How? It's simple. How can you feel like you suck at love when you have multiple men vying for your attention?

71.

You are in the driver's seat. You can go as fast or as slowly as you want.

The way things usually go is that we go out with the guy that asks us out. If we like him, we wait for him to ask us out again. We wait for the first kiss. We wait for him to put his arm around us or take our hand. If the relationship goes on long enough, we wait for him to say, "I love you." Eventually, we're waiting for him to propose. Why do we let the guy set the pace for the relationship? When you're dating multiple men, you're taking the wheel in your life. If you want to see someone again, ask them. If you feel like things are moving too quickly with someone, then tell them you can't see them because you have another date that night. The point is, with several different options of men to spend your time with, you will no longer be preoccupied with or at the mercy of one man's speed limit signs.

72.

You will feel more purposeful.

When you are only dating one guy at a time, you can feel a bit like you're just being swept along by the tide. Every difference of opinion is a potential source of conflict, and the relationship and all that it entails—the least of which is usually a great deal of time that you have invested—is at stake. For that reason, you may negotiate or compromise on things which, were the stakes different, you wouldn't. This may not seem like a big deal, but through one small concession at a time it is possible to stray utterly from your own personal path. You spend hours upon hours trying to convince someone to see it your way when really he should see it the way he sees it with someone who sees it like him and vice versa. But because you have put in so much time with him you feel the need to put in more. Time passes and, well, by then you are supposed to be only dating each other—or so you think. This doesn't happen when you're dating multiple men because your focus from the beginning is on you. You listen to yourself more. Your instincts guide you. You trust them. You realize that they move you into dates to teach you more about yourself and what you want. The guys have to fit in with and accommodate you. You maintain a sense of purpose and direction in your life as it pertains to the men you date.

73.

You will become fearless.

Some of you may be saying, "Sure, you're fearless; it's because you have nothing to lose!" But this is not at all the case. When you date multiple men you naturally cultivate a certain sense of detachment. I don't mean that you don't have emotional connections, or that you don't care about the men you are dating. What I mean is that you are not so emotionally entangled with a guy that you feel like what is happening to him is happening to you. This is important, because if you feel that your fate is tied to someone else and their life, then you feel powerless, and you don't even know why you feel that way. We don't have a clue why, when he says he is having a bad day, we all of a sudden start having a bad day too. Even if it's for a split second, if we say we like a guy and we have committed to date only him then, mentally, his day affects our day. But if you date widely, you never lose the ability to differentiate between who they are and who you are. You are not overly caught up in what they do or say, or the decisions they make, because you don't feel that it necessarily reflects on you. You are separate and distinct from them. You care, and if one of the guys you are dating expresses that he is facing a challenge then yes, you want it to get better; but you move on with your day. You are not obligated to bear their burdens or feel their pain. This is why you are fearless.

74.

You'll learn the meaning of the cliché, "There is power in numbers."

Is there such a thing as too many choices? If you're scrolling through satellite T.V. channels, maybe; but when it comes to who you're going to spend your time with, and who you choose to ultimately spend your life with, hell no there's no such thing as too many choices. The more men that you take the time to get to know a little bit, the more likely it is that you are going to find what you are looking for, even if you can't clearly articulate, in this moment, exactly what that is. And as a matter of fact, if you don't know exactly what you're looking for, then dating multiple men is the only way you're going to figure it out. You will not only encounter many different qualities that you can decide whether or not you like in a partner, you will also get to see how those qualities interface with your own, and how various different qualities work together within a single person. Would you walk into a shoe store that was only selling one size, style and color of shoe, purchase it without looking anywhere else, and walk out happy? I doubt it.

75.

You can finally live out the real life of the alter ego you keep hidden.

We all have one—the fantasy self that we're afraid to let out, that little-bit-of-bad girl that we think that the good guys, the marrying kind of guys, won't want to see in us. Ceasing to think in terms of potentially marrying every guy you go out with is like unlocking the prison door on this fantasy self. What's the worst that can happen? It's just one date, not an audition for marriage. And what do you have to gain by keeping some vital and important aspect of yourself imprisoned for most of your life? This is one of the reasons why carefully crafted marriages end, because one day that alter ego can no longer take being stifled anymore and she starts banging on her prison doors and yelling and screaming. Let her out to play! If you do end up meeting "the one," she deserves a place at the table, and this won't be a problem, because he'll already adore her.

76.

For the first time in your life you are making the dating rules, not your mom, or every other woman that held your hand as a young girl and explained what it meant to be a "good girl" and a "bad girl."

You're a grown woman. Does your mother still have a say in whether or not you wear makeup, or how long your skirts are? Then why should she or any other woman who has been an influence in your life get to tell you what you should or shouldn't do on a first date? Or how many men you should date? Or how many dates you should go on before you ought to be "going steady?" You don't let other people run your career or your household. Tell those voices from the past to shut up, and do what feels right to you. Defining "good" and "bad" for yourself doesn't make you a rebel or a disappointment; it makes you a philosopher. Like Beyonce says in one of my favorite songs called "Grown Woman"—I'm a grown woman, I can do whatever I want. You want to date multiple men, whether you're a "bad" girl or "good girl," just *Date, Girl!*

77.

If you see him out with another girl, so what? You can speak to him without wanting to cut his penis off.

We have all fallen into this trap. You go out with a guy, you hit it off, and you make plans to see each other again. Maybe you've even already had that second or third date. You're halfway down the aisle and he's . . . over there on the other side of the room in the company of another woman who is, quite obviously, a date. What the hell?! You call him every name in the book, and as far as you're concerned, it must be over. And it hurts because, well, things had been going so well. Once you start dating multiple men, you will never have this experience again. You probably won't notice him when your attention is focused on the fine-looking man sitting across from you because you are dating multiple men. And if you do notice him you won't care, and won't necessarily write him off as someone not to date again. He is still a viable candidate for a date because you'll have a different perspective on what is going on. When he sees you on your next date with him, he will wonder why your attitude is as welcoming as a flower in mid-bloom rather than an already dead one.

78.

You will no longer be the girl he calls for a date at the last minute.

Sure, being spontaneous is a great quality, but there's a difference between being the girl that's spontaneous and being the girl that's always there waiting for him because you have nothing else to do. THAT girl tends to get taken for granted. But when you are dating multiple men, he knows that you have value. Others want you, so you must be worth wanting. He will know that he is basically in competition for your time, and will step up his game accordingly. You only have to tell him one time that you already have a date and are not available for him to figure out that he had better give you some notice.

79.

You will have the courage to tell
that little voice in your head to
shut the hell up—it's only a
date, you aren't trying to marry
the guy.

That little voice. . . it tells us it's on our side, but
sometimes it's hard to be sure. You know the one I'm
talking about; the one that says, "You're laughing too
loud! He'll think you're faking it!" and, "Did you really
just tell him that? On a first date? He'll think you're a
nutcase!" and, "Look at those nose hairs; could you
really look at those nose hairs every day for the rest of
your life?" That little voice is your inner critic. It's the
fear and pressure that you carry around inside yourself
when you are focused on one single thing. It's the part
of you that's trying to shape events into what you want
them to be. No more. When you're dating multiple
men, your perspective changes. The little voice is no
longer in charge.

80.

You will stop picking men out of fear.

What if you end up with no one? It's a common fear—for women who only date one man at a time. Because when you're dating multiple men, your biggest problem is likely to be how to fit the men you'd like to date into your schedule, not that a man will never ask you out again. Once you have committed to dating whoever you want to, when you want to, you will attract other men into your life. For one thing, you will no longer be putting out the vibe that you are looking for "the one," which, quite frankly, can scare a lot of men away. You will be projecting a vibrant confidence, and you can choose who you want to spend your time with based on the qualities they present and how they make you feel, rather than out of fear.

81.

You will stop picking men out of insecurity.

When you are feeling insecure about yourself, you are vulnerable to the first guy that comes along with a compliment, a dinner, a movie and a couple of sweet nothings in your ear. Compliments are great, but the momentary lift that you get because someone says what you regard as all the right things to you doesn't mean that you are supposed to throw in the towel and give them all you've got. Yes, you are attracted to them, but that doesn't mean you have to give them the full ice cream and cake. When you think you have met "the one" but you know you are saying yes to him because you feel insecure at the prospect of meeting someone else anytime soon, I highly recommend taking the time and space to date multiple men. It is important if you only intend to date one man at a time, to know that you are not getting exclusively involved with someone only because they fill a hole in you that you ought to be filling up yourself. Now, if when you are first starting on this journey you pick men out of insecurity, so what? With your new philosophy, a date is just a date. If it works out and you like them, great. If not—you can go your separate ways, no harm, no foul. As you continue to date, your confidence will grow and insecurity will become a thing of the past.

82.

You will no longer compromise commitments you have made to yourself.

How many times have you said you were going to do something for you, and then backed out on yourself because a guy asked you out? Or because the guy you are dating exclusively had something else in mind for the evening? We women naturally gravitate towards putting others first in our lives—men, children, other family members. But when you make a commitment to start dating multiple men, you are moving yourself up your own priority list. You will no longer feel the pressure of obligation that can come with being in a monogamous relationship. What you do with your time, every day, is your choice. When you make a commitment to yourself, you will keep it.

83.

You'll stop putting up with men who do things that you don't like.

Relationships require negotiation, compromise, and sometimes sacrifice. These are not bad things, in and of themselves, but unfortunately it is all too easy to confuse them with, well . . . being something of a doormat. When you're only dating one man, the issue of property comes in. You have something, and it is a fact of human nature that most of us tend to want things to continue on as they are because life is easier and more comfortable when we know what to expect. Together these things create a kind of inertia. Sure, the man you are dating is always late. He calls waitresses "baby," and never cuts his toenails, and often disappoints you by not bothering to dress decently for a date. But he is yours, and for you that's all that matters. Well, no more. When you are dating multiple men, they need to show up and impress you. Period. And if they don't, you can move on to the next one.

84.

You will no longer compromise on your deal-breakers.

You know what these are; the things you absolutely refuse to live with in a relationship. Maybe they come from your childhood experiences, or maybe they're part of your inner architecture as a part of previous unsatisfactory relationships. Whatever their source, you are *serious* about not putting up with them . . . until you've been dating one guy for six months, and he suddenly starts presenting with one of these behaviors. Your first instinct may be to cut him loose right then and there, but then you start thinking. You've already invested *six months*. And everything else is good. Maybe you're being too sensitive. Maybe you're projecting old problems onto this relationship that aren't actually there. So you keep going. And so does the undesirable behavior. Screw that noise. When you're dating multiple men, your deal-breakers are your deal-breakers, and you honor yourself by walking away when they present themselves.

85.

You will become comfortable taking your time.

I've talked a lot in this book about how we ladies often respond to personal inner pressures, as well as family and societal expectations, and try to rush along from milestone to milestone in a relationship. But men can be guilty of this too, and sometimes, when you a meet a guy who is as anxious for a relationship as you are, it can be all too easy to get swept up in the promise and intensity and end up somewhere else, and not entirely sure how you got there. Dating multiple men changes the paradigm of relationships because you are no longer thinking in a straight line. It will teach you to slow down and to feel comfortable doing so. You may very well end up in an exclusive, monogamous relationship with one of the guys you are dating, eventually. But if you do, it will be on your terms and on purpose, and you will understand exactly how you got there.

86.

The power you feel from having choice is unbelievable.

We exercise choice when we vote, when we select an entrée from a menu, and when we style our hair. Hell, we even exercise choice when we buy toilet paper. Choice is the means by which we express ourselves in the world. When we have choice, and we exercise it, we exist. Every choice we make brings us into sharper focus, both to those around us and to ourselves. The absence of choice, in fact, is a mainstay in dystopian novels for a reason; it's because to not have choice is to not have power. Dating multiple men will make you feel powerful. Try it and see.

87.

You will stop obsessing over one man.

Obsessing over a man is not good for your health. It affects your sleep and your appetite. It can keep you keyed up, day and night, and distract you from other things that you could be doing. It takes the focus off of yourself, but not in a good way. You spend your time trying to figure out how to shape yourself into what you think he wants, rather than into what you want. And quite frankly, it's not fun. When you're dating multiple men, this otherwise chronic condition goes away. You think about the men you're dating, but those thoughts are spread out across several men, and your life doesn't revolve around any of them.

88.

You are not sitting around waiting on him to make things official.

When we're only dating one man, we can't help but think linearly. We're on a road, right? And roads, by definition, have destinations. This kind of thinking is so ingrained in us, in fact, that the idea of a relationship just being what it is, as opposed to it always being in the process of becoming something else, almost doesn't even make sense to us. So when we are dating a man, and not dating anyone else, and assuming he is doing the same, we are always waiting for that conversation about exclusivity and monogamy, and for permission to proudly use the word, "boyfriend." Forget about all of that. Why are we sitting around essentially waiting for someone else to validate us? When you're dating multiple men you don't have time to sit around waiting for anything, and you very quickly come to realize that you don't even want to.

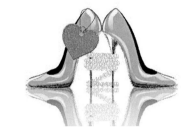

PART V: STOP SETTLING

Reasons 89 — 105

89.
You'll become a valuable asset.

It is a basic economic principle that scarcity plus demand creates value. When you are dating multiple men, you implement the same concept into your dating life. You become a "scarcity" for that man, which is a good thing. No man likes a woman who is always available for him at his beck and call. You are not sitting on a proverbial shelf, waiting for that "one guy" that you have decided you like a lot (and who likes you, but who doesn't want to "commit" right now) to ask you out. You are already out. When a man calls and gets your voice mail, that's scarcity. When it takes you six hours to answer his text, if you get to it that day at all, that's scarcity. Knowing that other men are interested in you, and have been able to secure your time, makes you valuable. Dating multiple men means getting yourself off the discount rack and into Tiffany's.

90.

You won't feel taken for granted.

When you are only dating one guy, you tend to focus on pleasing him. This can make him feel special, initially, which is a good thing, right? Well. . . yes . . . if he makes you feel special too. But if the guy is not putting the same effort into pleasing you, then two things begin to happen. The first, ironically, is that instead of talking to him about your feelings of disappointment and dissatisfaction, or indicating to him that you feel there is a lack of balance in the relationship, you start to try harder to please *him* because you don't want to rock the boat. You hypnotize yourself into believing subconsciously that if you just do a "lil bit" more, he will eventually come around and see that he needs to step it up. The second is that the things that you are doing for him no longer seem special; he begins to expect them. And there you are, being taken for granted. When you're dating multiple men this situation rarely plays itself out because you don't have enough time or interest to spoil a man that has not shown himself deserving. Plus, it's impossible to feel taken for granted when they are competing over *you*.

91.

You'll be less concerned about a guy's flaws because you don't have everything invested in this one guy.

When you don't allow yourself the freedom to date multiple men, it can be easy to start stewing over things that you don't like about a guy because, well, you feel stuck with them. You can end up continuously dealing with character traits that ultimately would be deal breakers. This stewing can be dangerous, and lead you down roads better left untraveled, like the "change a dude" road that I talk about in Reason # 33. When you date multiple men, though, not only are any one guy's flaws not as big of a concern for you, you also get to maintain a perspective on them. Different guys have different flaws, and some will be more egregious than others. And then you may come to find that something that initially drove you up a wall about a guy isn't that bad after all if he turns out to be "the one." You are less concerned about it because 1) you have both decided that you are ready to take it to another level and date exclusively; and (2) you discover that he really has no flaws: those old "flaws" are what you like most about him. With dating multiple men you see that what you thought were his flaws were really not all that big of a deal compared to the flaws of prior dates. Nobody's perfect. But if you date multiple men you give yourself the time you need to pick and choose what you are willing to live with.

92.

You aren't scared to ask the questions you really want to know the answers to.

When you are only dating one man, if you want to keep dating him you may be reluctant to ask certain questions. Yes, you want to know the answers; but you're also afraid of what the answers might be, so you just don't ask. This is an inherently unstable and unsatisfactory way to have a relationship, and it can be avoided. The solution is simple: don't get involved in an exclusive, monogamous relationship with any man unless those nagging questions have been asked and answered to your satisfaction. I do not understand how we were all tricked and bamboozled into doing this any other way. Why commit to one guy and then after you commit ask the hard questions? When you are dating multiple men, you feel comfortable asking the questions because you don't have so much at stake on the answers. And if the answers aren't what you want them to be, then you don't pursue the relationship. Problem solved.

93.

You'll enjoy how he makes you feel important.

When a guy wants to date you, and he knows you are dating multiple men, he will step up his game. Men like to say that they do not like the concept of anyone they like dating other people, and that may be true for some boys. But real men honor and respect a woman that honors herself enough to not give herself over to him without getting to know him first. The fact is that not enough women do it. Most women are so excited to have a man interested in them in any kind of way that they just hand it all over at "hello," or at latest usually 4 dates after. When a man knows a woman is not hell bent on just him, and that getting to know him is important to you, then he is more prone to always show up and make a conscious effort to give the best of who he is. A real man knows who he is and is not concerned initially with knowing there are other men interested in you or if you are comparing them to him. A real man is only concerned with making you feel important at whatever level you are in the dating process, in hopes that should he get to ultimately have you all to himself, those other guys you compared him to will be a non-factor. Not only that—you are dating, not playing house. A real man ultimately wants a woman that understands her worth and knows that there are levels to dating. He understands that he should be holding doors open for you, and bringing you flowers, or whatever he feels he needs to do to make a girl feel special. He listens to you say what you like and enjoys doing the things for you that make you smile. And if he doesn't? Then move on, because someone else will be happy to make you feel important.

94.

You'll never have to look at
yourself in the mirror again,
knowing that you have lowered
the bar.

Can I get an Amen! Chile, we've all done it—committed
ourselves too early and then stayed with someone way
too long, beyond when it became clear that there were
issues, because everything else outside of those
"issues" was going well. It is very, very difficult to end
a relationship especially when it is going well on a
number of levels, but is just not *enough*. You may not
even be able to articulate what exactly is wrong. You
just know certain things he says makes you unsettled
from the inside. We stay. Everything seems okay from
the outside, but we know we have lowered the bar. We
diminish what we know is going on inside of us telling
us this is not the one. We question our feelings of being
unsettled. We judge our standards and throw them out
the windows like trash and make ourselves believe that
we are asking for too much. When you are dating
multiple men, this doesn't have to happen because
there is no commitment, either actual or implied. There
is no pressure to commit until both of you agree that
the "datingship" is ready to move to that level. You

don't have to continue to see someone that isn't right for you, and you don't have to "break up" with them, either. Moving on is as simple as declining a date—two or three times if you have to.

95.

You can stop lying to yourself that the guy you have put up with for the last two years is "the one."

Making it one, or two, or even twenty years through a relationship does not necessarily mean that you have found your soul mate. It doesn't necessarily mean that you are lying to yourself either; but dating multiple men will remove the possibility of you having to convince yourself that someone you are dating exclusively is "the one," just on the basis of exclusivity itself. In fact, until your relationship with one particular guy emerges as something significant to you, you should not contemplate the concept of "the one" at all with any of the guys you are dating. The concept of finding "the one" interrupts your ability to simply experience the date for what it is at this moment with the person you are with and how that makes you feel. It is very easy to be honest with yourself about how you feel about someone you are dating when you are dating several men. For one thing, you have a better perspective on each of them as a result of the juxtaposition. For another, you won't get to the point of having to justify the time you have invested because as soon as you start to feel that you are only "putting up with" the guy, you end the relationship, quickly and cleanly.

96.

You won't think a guy is the right guy just because he's the only guy in your life.

If you are in a relationship and there are problems, then there are problems. Relationship problems are not exclusive to one-on-one relationships. Dating multiple men doesn't mean that you will never end up spending time with a guy who judges you, or who can't communicate, or who doesn't make you feel like a priority. The difference is that when you get into an exclusive relationship with one guy who even you know is not as into you as you are to him, you tend to make excuses for these things because you want it to work, and when you date multiple men, you don't. Listen to me closely, the fact that you and one guy have made a commitment to see each other exclusively doesn't mean that you should see each other exclusively. What are his actions? Does he treat you like you want to be treated? Avoid the problem entirely by not making that exclusivity commitment in the first place unless your gut tells you that he is the right guy, and the feeling is mutual. Pay attention to your gut.

97.

You won't stay in a relationship longer than you ought to.

Most marriages are the inevitable conclusion of an exclusive, monogamous relationship that both parties have decided to make permanent. It is a fact that about half of all marriages end in divorce, and divorce is messy, confrontational, painful and expensive. But the problem in many cases wasn't the marriage; it was that the relationship that preceded it was taken too far. When you are dating multiple men, when things stop working you let them go. It's that simple. Period point blank. The end. In order to make it to exclusivity and monogamy, you and one particular guy need to go through a lot of issues and over a lot of hurdles. Dating multiple guys, you will tend to want to spend more time with one of them. That is expected and is okay. That will mean that you hopefully are talking and getting to know each other better. But you are still not exclusive with him. Hopefully you reach some bumps in the road too. These bumps in the road and disagreements as you are dating are like an insurance policy against divorce; it greatly reduces the chances of you rushing into an exclusive, monogamous relationship that is going to sweep you along into a doomed marriage to begin with. You don't take commitment lightly, so chances are that when you make one, it will be the right one.

98.

You'll ask yourself if the things he does and says really make you happy, instead of simply accommodating yourself to them.

When you are in an exclusive relationship with a guy, you want it to be a good one, right? Of course you do! Which is why, when you are with a guy who is really trying, who really makes an effort, you tend to stay, even if what he is doing doesn't really feel right. After all, he's trying; if you're not happy, doesn't that just make you hard to please? No. It makes you human. If you're not clicking, you're not clicking. When you are dating multiple men you don't have to pretend that just because he is trying that what he's doing is right for you. It's either right or it's not. When it is, you keep seeing him. When it's not, you cut him loose, and you don't feel bad about it. Trust me, ladies; the men you are dating are making these same kinds of decisions about you. They are more than likely dating multiple women while they are getting to know you, even if they are not saying it.

99.

A few dates with one guy does not mean that you are off the market, attached, and should stop seeking or being sought by another.

Committing yourself to one person is a big deal. It's a much bigger deal than we usually make of it. While you can know a lot about a person after a few dates, you're still really only scratching the surface. A person's true character can only be revealed over time, and many, many interactions. And you certainly don't really know someone until you've seen them under pressure. And yet, time and time again, we meet someone, like what we see, and basically offer them the rest of our lives. Dating multiple men changes this paradigm. It means that you are giving yourself the gift of time in which to make a wise and sound decision that ultimately will affect almost every aspect of your life.

100.

You don't commit to something that is only there in your imagination.

Human beings have a profound need for emotional, physical and spiritual connection. It is part of our wiring. We look for connection everywhere. We spiderweb our world with connections—we connect to songs, to movies or books, or places; we see ourselves reflected in a certain animal, or a certain color, or a certain cause; we use Instagram, Facebook, Twitter, Periscope and LinkedIn and we connect, connect, connect . . . is it any wonder that we place so much weight on what we hope and expect to be the most profound connection of our lives? Our need to make a connection with a significant other is so strong that we often project one even when it is not really there. Social media—the "show and tell" lives that we get sucked into—paints a picture that everything happens in an instant. We want it now and yesterday. Marriages and families can be built on these phantom connections, which can last for decades before finally revealing themselves for what they are. Dating multiple men is not a lack of connection; it simply means that you are putting each connection that you make into the proper perspective. Some of them will grow and deepen; others won't. You're allowing yourself the time—not your imagination—to be able to tell the difference.

101.

You will stop giving your gift of monogamy away.

Monogamy—which is to say, the gift of yourself—is the most precious gift that you have to give. It is to say to someone that they are enough for you, that of all the people in existence, "I choose you. I choose to go to that next level of dating with *you*." What are you basing your choice on? For many of us, our choice is based on little more than circumstance and convenience. This is crazy! Think of it this way. Would you invite someone to move in with you, and put their name on the deed to your house after three dates? Of course you wouldn't. When you date multiple men you will gain a better perspective on monogamy. You'll see it for the immensely profound and valuable gift that it is, and you'll want to cherish and protect it, rather than giving it away—and basing your decision on "feelings" that you have—to a man that has not shown himself deserving.

102.

Quantity will eventually get you quality.

There are quality men out there, and if you haven't found one yet, then you haven't looked at enough of them. For one thing, dating multiple men will teach you what quality is. Most of us don't need to date multiple men to be able to tell the really good dude from the asshole, but we do need experience and practice to be able to tell Mr. Almost from Mr. Hell Yes! The biggest problem with committing to one guy too soon is that you can't be sure that he's not just Mr. Almost. Think of it like panning for gold. You don't pick a single pebble up out of a stream bed and declare it gold just because it shines when the light hits it. You rake up pan after pan after pan from the riverbed and sift through it all until you find the one or two flakes of real gold.

103.

You will no longer be the only one committing to a relationship.

This is a problem that often arises when all of our focus is on dating just one man. It begins when women mistake half a dozen dates with one particular guy for a "relationship" in the first place. Dating multiple men removes the possibility that you will make the assumption that you are the only woman another guy is dating because, well, you're dating other people yourself. Furthermore, you have told him so. You can't end up in an accidental or imaginary relationship because according to the parameters you have clearly laid out, moving from "dating" to a "relationship" necessitates a conversation in which both of you agree that dating exclusively is a step that you want to take with each other. Therefore there are no assumptions, no misunderstandings, and no imaginary boyfriends.

104.

Real men like to work for things. Make him work for your attention.

You may have heard the advice that a woman should "play hard to get." It's classic dating strategy—and for very good reasons. I agree in essence, but with a slight change or adjustment. First, it does give you time to really see if you are more than just physically attracted to him. Secondly, it gives a man time to decide whether or not he really actually wants you, or if his interest was just in passing. A man that does not work for you in the beginning ultimately sets the foundation for the relationship. Somehow time and society has convinced women that the attention needs to be equal. Wrong! If he really actually wants you, then he will work for you. And trust me, ladies, you only want a man that wants you. Thirdly, a woman who holds back her affections is being wise and honest, not "playing hard to get," which is my slight adjustment. She is smart enough to protect herself, and if she does not protect herself, then who will? A woman whose affections are difficult to attain does play to a man's ego. If and when he actually secures her affections, he feels that he is better than the other guys who were vying against him. He has won, and she is the prize. Can you play to a man's ego by making him work for your attention one guy at a time? Yes and no. You can certainly make yourself unavailable without actually dating other guys, and put the poor guy through his paces in the same way that you would check out a horse to ensure that he is sound, strong, healthy, and of a good temperament before you buy him. But then you can be accused of merely playing games, and rightly so. If you are genuinely seeing other people then you don't have to play games. He will naturally be forced to work for your attention, and if he really likes you, he will.

105.

You will learn to only give loyalty when it is deserved.

I used the word "deserve" in this instance assuming that you honestly believe in your heart that you deserve loyalty. I believe that is why you give your loyalty away so easily and freely. Maybe you cannot define when someone deserves your loyalty? Maybe that is difficult for you. On the other hand, it's not hard to define when they don't deserve it. Usually situations in which someone doesn't deserve it involve lying, cheating, and all those other buzz words that are obviously usually deal breakers. We give our loyalty to men who are nice to us. But just because someone is a nice person and you don't want to hurt their feelings doesn't mean that you should continue to see them. Neither do you owe them your loyalty just because you've been together for a long time, or because you once had romantic feelings for them, even though now you don't. It's selling yourself short to remain loyal to someone that you are with because you don't think that you can do any better. And it's unfair to the person you're with if you're only being loyal to him because of the lifestyle or advantages that he can offer you. Dating multiple men will keep you from falling into any of these traps. It will also help you to define what it means to deserve *your* loyalty. Defining it will make it clearer to you why you should not just give it away so freely. When you get to know many different guys, you will figure out which ones deserve your loyalty and why, and you will only give it when it is deserved.

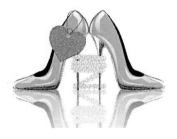

PART IV: THE ICING ON THE CAKE

Reasons 106 – 143

106.

You will learn to trust your gut.

One of the biggest problems with having a list of qualities that you want to find in a man is that you might actually find them. . .and instead of feeling elated as your relationship progresses, you feel an impending sense of doom. He's got the right education, the right job, the right attitude; he does sweet, spontaneous things for you. He helps you move. He babysits your dog. He has charmed your mother. But being with him just doesn't feel right. When you're dating multiple men, you're less likely to commit to Mr. Supposedly Perfect because you'll also be seeing other people who, sure, may be less perfect on paper, but with whom you *feel* better. You'll have the confidence to trust your gut and let Mr. Supposedly Perfect go so that he can find the woman that's perfect *for him*.

107.

It's fun to meet someone in the
frozen foods section of Whole
Foods—and be free to follow up
on it.

I know what you are saying: "Why is meeting a man in
the frozen food section at Whole Foods a reason that I
should date multiple men, Stacii Jae?" I hear you loud
and clear. Here you go. For me, meeting a man at a
grocery store represents the freedom that I believe
single girls should give themselves to enjoy
singlehood, flow and have fun. Meeting anyone at a
grocer is unconventional; it's not routine; it's outside of
the box. Routines keep us focused and on track, and
they do provide us with security. These are all very
good things, but they have a flip side, especially when
we're talking about routines as a single girl. The same
ole same. You do not have to follow the regime of
getting dressed up to go somewhere special with your
other single girls to meet someone. He can be right
there in the frozen food section at Whole Foods or any
of your local grocers. Whole Foods is where I shop.
Where do you shop? Go to the frozen food section
around 7 p.m.. Trust me. He may be there grabbing his
easy pop-in meal for the evening. Think about this.

What if you adopted the point of view that there are endless possibilities in your day to meet someone new just by leaving the house every day? Routines can lead to ruts, which is to say, boredom and frustration. Being single should be an exciting time for you. You have the opportunity to meet and date multiple men, and to ultimately find, during that process, the man you were born to be with for the rest of your life. You cannot get to that place as long as your life is in a cycle of making premature decisions to date one person for long periods of time that take you off the dating scene. The relationship does not work, you are single again. Another cycle starts. Dating multiple men will not only keep you from getting into a relationship too quickly, it will also leave room for spontaneity in your life. Spontaneity is good for you. There's nothing quite as romantic and exciting as a chance encounter in an unlikely place. Letting the sparks fly, and giving yourself the space and freedom to follow up on that moment, is empowering.

108.

Dating more than one guy at a time is more fun.

Dating multiple guys will make you feel great about yourself because there is so much interest in you, and when you feel good about yourself, you are automatically open to enjoying your life more. Making the decision to just date casually relieves a lot of the pressure that you are likely to put on yourself, and him, if you meet a guy and begin dating him exclusively before you really know him. You will inevitably want that guy to fill a void that he may not be able to fill. Dating multiple guys creates less pressure, which means that you will be more relaxed. And when you're not under pressure, you're much more likely to enjoy yourself. And why shouldn't you? You will be treated well because guys will be trying to outdo each other to impress you. You will spend more time out around people. You will have new experiences. You will begin to see fewer pitfalls, traps and disappointments in life and more opportunities and pleasures.

109.
You get tell him no because you have company.

If you have ever sat at home on a Friday or Saturday night because a guy you have been dating regularly hasn't initiated any plans with you, or if you have ever accepted a date at the last minute even though you knew in your gut that it was lowering your value, then I don't need to explain what's so great about this reason. Of course you're going to be up front with the guys you are seeing and tell them that you are seeing other people. But if he never sees or feels the impact of this, then how are you supposed to reap all of the supposed benefits of dating multiple men that I've been talking about in this book? Don't hide the fact that you already have plans when a guy calls you. Take his call, and let him know that you would have loved to see him, but you have made other plans. Yes, tell him why you can't accept his invitation. Tell him in your sweetest voice. Be the most beautiful rainbow after the roughest thunderstorm. Trust me. You dropping that detail will be a thunderstorm for him. Then watch what happens.

110.

You won't pass up other
opportunities for six months
while you're trying to figure out
whether or not you like one
particular guy, who probably
isn't the right guy for you
anyway.

Why should you limit yourself to one guy when you
haven't really figured out whether or not you like him?
Limiting yourself to one guy at a time only invites
pressure into your life, both from yourself and
potentially from well-meaning family and friends.
There's no good reason to do this when you can figure
it out while dating several guys at the same time. Not
to mention how it makes you feel when you start into
a relationship with one guy after another only to see it
fail or fall to pieces or, ultimately, make you miserable.
And in the meantime, years of your life are going by.
Stop passing up opportunities and start living. You
have absolutely no risk and nothing to lose.

111.

You don't have to be disappointed.

There are *so* many ways to get disappointed when you are only seeing one guy at a time. These range from being disappointed over little things that he does or doesn't do, all the way up to the ultimate disappointment of having invested so much of yourself and so much time in your life into a relationship that just isn't right. Remember Reason #50. Expectations and disappointment go hand in hand. When you are dating multiple men you may still occasionally get disappointed, but the impact is going to be far less than if you were only dating one man. The wound, if there is one, will be shallow and heal quickly. And you can take each disappointment in stride, confident that whatever "loss" you may be suffering is merely your life restructuring itself to make room for something better.

112.

You can have a man for each of your personalities.

I have talked in other reasons about being completely honest, and about indulging your secret alter ego, and I absolutely stand behind all of these suggestions. But when you're dating multiple men, there's no hurry to reveal all of yourself to each of them. You set the pace. You control the timing of if and when you allow the opportunity to them to get to know all of you. But, if you love to dance, then you can do that with the guy who also loves to dance, and still enjoy a quiet stroll in the park with the quiet guy who appeals to your introspective and philosophical side. One day you will find a guy whose own multi-faceted personality is totally in sync with your own. And that one there may be "the one" because of that. But until you do, there's no need to be in a relationship with one person who does not appreciate all aspects of what makes you *you*. There is no reason that you should have to pick and choose which aspect of yourself you need to present to someone because that works for him. Dating multiple men means you can enjoy them all, in the company of several men who enjoy them too.

113.

You can wear your favorite "Go get 'em, girl!" outfit more.

We all have one—the perfect outfit—the one that makes us feel confident, sexy, and powerful. The only thing wrong with this outfit, in fact, is that once he's seen it, we can't wear it again too soon. No more! Remember, dating multiple men is about you and how you feel. You can keep going out with new guys for as long as you want to, which means you can wear that awesome outfit for "the first time" with every one of them. I know it sounds silly. And it is. But there is some truth to it, especially when you are on a budget. LOL. This not only means that you will continue to feel really good about yourself, it is also likely to save you money. You won't be tempted to outdo yourself buying something new like you would if every date was with the same guy.

114.

You will receive more compliments.

This really speaks for itself. But I will add that getting compliments on a date from a guy who is clearly expressing romantic interest in you isn't the same as getting a compliment from a co-worker or from your mother. Moreover, dating multiple men gives you an opportunity to receive a wider range of compliments. I say, date three men. That is the magic number for me. There are going to be some that see things in you that other guys have not seen, and that maybe even you have never seen before. You will not just feel appreciated, you will feel appreciated on whole new levels. You will learn things about yourself—good things—that will both increase your confidence and help you to understand yourself better.

115.

It's okay if he's boring, because you don't have to listen to him every night.

Not literally so boring that you fall asleep on the date, or even that you are not interested in what he is saying; when I say boring, I actually mean his conversation may not be as interesting to you as the conversation of others. If you agree to go out with him in the first place, there has to be a reason, right? Maybe he is fantastically good-looking. Maybe he has the financial wherewithal to take you to places you would never otherwise be able to go. Or maybe you can't even put a finger on what it is that made you say yes, there was just something about him that interested you enough to make you think that he was worth your effort to get to know. And then when you are actually on the date, you realize that he's a bore and talks about nothing but himself. He's putting you to sleep. So what? Order the lobster and a second margarita and let him drone on. If he's good-looking, then enjoy looking at him and tune him out. If you choose, this can be the last night you'll ever have to listen to him.

116.

It's okay if he's a vegetarian,
because the guy you're going
out with on Wednesday is a
meat eater.

When you're dating several guys at the same time,
you'll encounter different desirable qualities in each
one. Likewise, you'll probably discover things about
each one that you aren't thrilled about. But when you
accept the fact that a date is just a date, and not
necessarily a prelude to a relationship, then the things
that don't thrill you don't necessarily have to be deal-
breakers. Dating multiple men gives you an
opportunity to enjoy all the nuances that people have
to offer without having to accept any of them
permanently into your life, unless you want to. If you
are dating just one man at a time, and that man is a
vegetarian, that situation may make you envision a
lifetime of tofu and bean sprouts on your dinner plate.
And rightfully so. But when it's just one date with just
one guy who just so happens to be a vegetarian, whom
you may or may not ever see again, who cares? Dating
widely gets you out of the habit of automatically
assuming that you are going to have to become what
he is in order for you to get along for the long term.

117.

You'll save on groceries because your robust dating life means more dinners out.

This is a great reason to date multiple men, especially if you don't like to cook. Not only will you not have to go to the grocery store as often, you will also probably enjoy your leftover meals more than if you had cooked them on your own. And if you do like to cook? Well, you get an advantage, there, too. Rather than having to spend your money on keeping your kitchen stocked with the staples, you can shop and splurge at the grocer on the fancy stuff, or on your favorites. There will be more dinners out, so when you are dining in you have the freedom to explore creating new and fancy dishes for yourself that you normally would not splurge on. Freeing up money in your grocery budget can also mean more money for clothes, or a standing mani-pedi appointment, or money to go towards your annual vacation.

118.

You will always have someone to ask when you need some kind of help.

Guys like to fix things, and different guys have different skills. Say you're dating one guy who is a lawyer, and another guy who understands how electrical things work, and a third guy who can cook. You have a pool of free, skilled labor at your fingertips. As men pass into and out of your life, the skill sets at your disposal will change. When you are dating multiple men, one of them will usually be able to help you with some particular problem that you have in your life. And getting a flat tire is such a common thing, odds are one in any three guys will be able to change it for you.

119.

You get to date all the WRONG guys.

Yes, yes, I know—this is supposed to entice you? But bear with me for a second; I have a point to make. When you finally do settle down with someone, how are you supposed to fully appreciate what you have and know for sure that he's the right guy? I've talked a lot about how dating multiple men will help you to sort through the nuances of personality to find the right fit, but this reason is about the big things, and being thankful for the kind of guy that you don't commit to: the mama's boy; the clingy guy; the guy who wants to be your best friend so much that somehow he ceases to seem masculine; the overgrown boy; or the man who is already married to his career. If you date enough men before choosing one to commit to, you're bound to run into all of these guys—briefly. While dating multiple guys you can learn what you can about what you don't want, and move the hell on.

120.

You won't marry your rebound guy.

The rebound relationship is great at first. How could it not be? After all, your rebound guy is usually your anti-ex; he's everything you wanted in a guy but didn't have before. But slow down, because you were with your ex for a reason. He obviously had some qualities that were important to you, or you wouldn't have been with him for so long. Though you're likely to be smitten at first, over time, a rebound relationship will reveal its shallowness and ultimately become unsatisfactory. But it has served its purpose; it's gotten you back out there. It's proved that you can, in fact, be attractive to another man. If you're just getting out of a long-term relationship, now is the perfect time to make a commitment to yourself to date multiple men. Do not, I say *do not* commit to one guy when you are just getting out of a long term relationship. Enjoy your rebound guy; hell, enjoy dating two or three of them at the same time. It's your prerogative.

121.

You'll get more of your needs fulfilled.

Different guys fulfill different needs. And until you find the one guy that can fulfill all of them, if such a guy even exists, there's no reason why you should have to pick and choose which of your needs gets met for a year or two at a time as you move into and out of different monogamous relationships. When you are dating multiple men, you can get all of your needs fulfilled. You can have one "friend" that you call when you feel like snuggling on the sofa and watching a movie with subtitles. You can have another that takes you to trendy nightclubs when you feel like a night on the town. A third guy may be the perfect person to confide in. No need to pick and choose when you can have them all. That is, until the day comes that one out of the three stands out and he is the one that can fulfill all your needs—or at least the ones that are most important to you. Now remember, dating multiple guys does not mean that you are having sex with multiple guys at the same time. In fact, I recommend not sleeping with anyone until you make a decision that you want to stop dating three and date that special one that you like.

122.

You are free to pursue
opportunities as they arise.

The typical woman stays in an exclusive relationship when she is ultimately not happy. She continues to make endless attempts to have conversations with her mate, hoping that the relationship will get better, and that he will change. However, just because she is dating a guy exclusively doesn't necessarily mean that she is not interested in other guys, or that she doesn't occasionally have the desire to pursue an opportunity. My confusion is this: if she feels that way, then why is she dating anyone exclusively at all? More than likely, the chances of anything getting better in the exclusive relationship to which she is giving all of her time and energy are slim to none. You can date more than one guy at a time and still continue to date that one guy for whom you have all this hope, as long as you're being honest about it. For example, say you are at the bar having a texting a conversation with the one guy on whom you have pinned all your hopes. You hate texting and have explained that to him. Yet, he continues to text. A handsome man sits down next to you, orders a cognac, and sends you a drink. If you are not tied down, and since you hate the back and forth of texting anyway, you can tell the guy texting you that you have to go, you'll chat tomorrow, and turn your attention to the handsome stranger.

123.

Your life will become fun and exciting.

Exciting is when you never know what's coming next—in a good way. When you're dating multiple men, romantic potential lies around every corner. You're more likely to take time with your clothes and makeup no matter where you go, which means you will both project confidence and look attractive, so you will draw people to you. You will spend more time out around people, and less time nuking frozen meals in the microwave and eating over the sink in your sweats. You'll become more familiar with where you live, and discover new, great things to do there. You may learn new things or pick up a new hobby. Your life becomes a source of infinite possibility.

124.

You never again have to hear, "I need some space."

Psychologists may say that "needing space" is not necessarily a sign of rejection, but when you're really into a guy and he tells you he "needs some space," it sure feels like the brush-off. This doesn't happen when you are dating multiple guys, because you don't see any of them often enough to make them feel claustrophobic with you. Not only that, you're not pressuring them to see you more, or about where things are "going," so they don't feel the need to slow down or pull away. You're not offended or freaked out if he doesn't ask you out one weekend, because if you want to go out at all, there's others you can go out with. In fact, you're probably having the exact opposite effect on a guy who really likes you; he's going to want to see you more. When you're dating multiple men, if anyone needs some space, girl, it's you!

125.

It's great to have options.

One of the great things about dating different guys at the same time, and having new people constantly coming into your life, is that your options expand. This reason isn't so much about the different guys themselves being your options as it is about the many and various options that the guys bring into your life. You may learn about a great new restaurant, or your city's best kept hole-in-the-wall secret chili place. Who has the best fried lobster? Someone you are dating may hook you up with a great new job opportunity or, if you are an entrepreneur, introduce you to someone who may turn out to be a new business client. When you date multiple men, your world, your network and your options are always growing. And let's not forget that that the wider the net, the better the opportunities are that you can meet other men, men who may be better for you, and whom you would not have met otherwise.

126.

You can buy a dress that you'd like to see yourself in, rather than one you think he'd like to see you in.

How are you ever going to meet a guy who appreciates and shares your tastes if you're always giving in to someone else's? When you date multiple men you will stop outfitting yourself to please one guy, and focus on pleasing yourself. The freedom to choose your own clothes without wondering or caring what someone else will think about them is one of the perks of both being yourself and making yourself happy. If a guy criticizes or rejects your clothes, then he is criticizing or rejecting you. Wear what *you* want! Let this be one of the ways that you figure out which guys to keep, and which to cut loose. And as for whether or not he will be pleased, remember—we don't always know we want something until someone shows us that it is possible.

127.

You will no longer lose hair from being stressed out over a dude.

The biggest source of stress in a relationship is whether or not it will continue. Dating multiple men can help to relieve this stress in two ways. The first, obviously, is that you have made no commitment to make your relationship permanent in the first place, so whether or not any particular dating relationship will endure is of no concern to you. But that aside, the overarching principles of dating multiple men that I have laid down in this book – honesty, being yourself, asking the difficult questions while there is relatively little to lose – will help you hang onto your hair if and when a relationship does develop, too. Because at that point you will have already made your deal-breakers known. You will already know if he really likes you for who you are. You will know if he is willing to do anything to be your everything. And the situation will be without sarcasm, criticism, or judgement because you wouldn't have gotten this far otherwise. You will have exercised a conscious choice while you have power, autonomy and hair.

128.

You'll start to date up.

Do you date who you want to date or what you honestly believe in your heart you deserve? I know it is a horrible thing to say, but I believe sometimes we date who we feel will date us. Usually it is a type of guy that we feel comfortable with because he is the "type" that we are used to dating. Out of every ten guys we date, seven are generally the same type physically, economically and socially. But have you ever asked yourself if this is really the guy you want? Is he really the type you want? Have you ever seen a so-so man out with a gorgeous woman and wondered, why is *she* with *him*? Is he fabulously wealthy? Does he "make her laugh?" Maybe. Men tend to accept who they are and what they look like, and go after what they want, and self-confidence is attractive. As you date multiple men, you will gain confidence in yourself. You'll see enough of what you don't want, both on the macro and micro levels, to be motivated to go after what you do want, rather than just being content with only the "type" you have been comfortable with dating in the past. You'll stop thinking that this or that guy is too handsome or too charming for you, and start to date your true worth.

129.

You'll look and feel younger.

Being in a committed but not-quite-right relationship, especially one to which you have committed too soon, can make you feel, well . . . old. Stale routines, predictable arguments and continually stifled frustrations can literally take years off of your life. Not to mention that as we get older our choices in life grow narrower because we grow more fearful to leave that relationship. The fear of not knowing what is on the other side makes most women stay. Dating multiple men, on the other hand, takes those years off figuratively instead. Anything is possible. You will take better care of your appearance, and you will pursue your own interests fearlessly and with the same uncompromising passion that you did when you were just starting out. Once you make a commitment not to limit yourself, you can remain an idealist until your ideal man appears.

130.

You'll feel more attractive.

No matter how good you feel about yourself, there is something very special you feel when a guy tells you that you're gorgeous. It is undeniably in the top five things a woman likes to hear from a man. And for some women, how he thinks she looks ranks above the opinion of anyone else, including the mirror. And honestly, that's okay. It's okay to admit that you desire and enjoy attention from the opposite sex. I know that I am an attractive girl. My confidence is on ten trillion, trust me. But it definitely does not hurt to hear it from someone outside of myself. You don't have to be a supermodel to feel like a supermodel. Date three. Over time, whether you are already confident or not, you will notice a change in the way you feel when you are in a room with men. You do feel more attractive. More desired. More wanted. So start dating them, and let them give your ego a boost.

131.

You'll dance more.

I love to dance. Dancing brings me unspeakable joy. For me it's expression. But none of the guys with whom I have ever had long relationships have enjoyed dancing. Weird, right? I'm not dancing every night, but knowing I have the opportunity to go out dancing with someone makes me very happy. If dancing makes you feel sexy, powerful and alive, it is disheartening to date a guy that doesn't like to dance. Dating multiple men will help you to get your boogie back on. You can date a guy for no other reason than that he likes to dance with you. Or maybe you'll discover that *not* liking to dance is one of your deal-breakers. If it's not dance for you, what activity do you enjoy, but do not get the opportunity to do when you are in a relationship with someone? Metaphorically speaking, what is your "dance?" However your particular dating scenarios work out, when you're dating multiple men, if you want to "dance," there is a guy available who wants to "dance" with you.

132.

You'll laugh more.

There are proven health benefits to laughing. When we laugh, we breathe in more oxygen, which is good for our organs. Laughter releases endorphins. And it activates and relieves the stress response in our bodies, leaving us feeling more relaxed. What does this have to do with dating multiple men? Men love to make us laugh, and there's nothing better than a man with a sense of humor. Humor comes in many flavors. Like ice cream, why pick just one? It's so easy to get sidetracked when dating; to get carried away by things like "commitment" and "direction" and "progress" and forget that both you and the guy are there to have fun! So accept dates. Enjoy yourself. Let all kinds of guys try to make you laugh. Think of it as therapy.

133.

You'll be more open to adventure.

Adventure doesn't have to mean climbing mountains. It can mean going to a new museum, or drinking beer in a dive bar. It can mean kayaking, or bicycling in the park. If you've never done it before, and you're not sure how it's going to turn out, it's an adventure. You are much more likely to do new things when dating multiple men because the fact of having decided to do it in the first place means that you are open to new experiences, and you are sending out a vibe that's inviting new experiences into your life. Try this, and you'll soon find that you've turned the tables on the dating game. What once used to stress you out—not knowing how things were going to turn out—becomes a desirable quality.

134.

If you're a person that likes to read, you will read more, etc.

Dating multiple men gets your focus off of a guy and onto yourself, where it belongs. Not in a bad way, but in the sense that you will stop giving up parts of yourself because they don't fit cleanly into an "us." You won't give up your after-work jog because your boyfriend likes to hit the happy hours. It won't take you forever to finish a novel because you can only really relax and read when you're alone. And although you are dating multiple guys, you choose when you want to be bothered and when you don't. So you can read more. Dating multiple guys doesn't mean that you are always in the rat race of dating differently people constantly, 365 days in a year. Absolutely not. Dating multiple men, you are in control. You'll make, and keep, dates with yourself. And you will gravitate towards and seek out people with whom you can enjoy reading; someone who likes the same things that you do. You'll be doing more of what you want to do, when you want to do it, and when you feel like doing it with someone, you'll be able to enjoy your favorite thing with someone else who enjoys it too.

135.

You'll stop being a drama queen.

You *hate* drama queens, and of course you never want to be one. But the assumptions and misunderstandings and false starts of a relationship can get intense. And when you're putting all of your energy into hoping something is going to work out with someone that you really hardly know and with whom you are fundamentally incompatible, the stresses can get the best of you. Your insecurity, disappointment, high hopes, hurt feelings, anger and unending frustration can leak out of you in words and looks that may make him feel like you're a bit too much to handle. Dating multiple men will relieve this pressure because you will stop trying so hard. You'll learn to take things as they come, to appreciate things when they are going well, and to let things go when they aren't.

136.

You'll stop picturing your wedding after three dates with a guy.

Trust me, when you start dating multiple men, your focus is no longer going to be on your wedding. You stop dating with the end in mind. When we spend a lot of time alone, it's easy to start to fantasize about that perfect guy who's going to show up one day and sweep us off our feet. The more time we spend not in a relationship and pining for one, the higher our expectations are when we do meet someone and start dating. It's all too easy to project onto them what we want them to be, or to assume the things that we don't like will change. When you're only dating one guy, you can usually fool yourself into getting into trouble, too, by convincing yourself that a certain guy is your husband. The more guys you date casually, though, the farther you get from those idealistic and premature fantasies. The thought of prematurely picking just one of the guys to be the only guy for you starts to seem, well, ridiculous. After all the years of doing just that, you finally see where you went wrong in all of your prior dating escapades. What's the old saying? You stop putting the cart before the horse. Plus, if you're not distracted by that wedding dress, you might see sooner rather than later that you do not even like the guy, and outside of his fancy car and his nice suit, all you have in common is—well, not much of anything.

137.

You'll learn things.

There is no end to what you will learn, both about yourself, about others and about the world. You'll not only learn what kinds of qualities in other people irritate you, and what makes you happy, and things like that; you'll also learn your own true worth and stop settling for less than you deserve. You'll learn that other people put themselves first, and that unless you take care of you, no one else is likely to do it for you. You'll also learn that people can surprise you, and that goodness has depths and facets which you may have never considered before. You'll learn the difference between things like infatuation and obsession and love. And you'll learn that nothing is self-sustainable. Dating multiple men is fun and liberating, but it's also full of priceless life lessons that you won't want to miss.

138.

You'll understand man's nature better.

You might want to argue that dating just one man will help you to understand that one man's nature better, but I'm not talking particulars, here; I'm talking generalities. I'm not talking about one man; I'm talking about mankind. Understanding how men think, and how that translates into behavior will help you to get along with men better. When you date multiple men, you'll start to realize what things are just a man being a man, and what things are aspects of a unique personality. This will save you a great deal of aggravation over time, since you will stop fighting things that you can't win. You'll start to realize that all the begging, pleading, screaming and yelling in the world isn't going to change a man's basic nature, and you won't waste your time or your energy trying to do it.

139.

You'll become a more well-rounded woman.

Most people tend to do the same things in the same way. Over and over again. For months that can become years that can become decades. Dating multiple men gets you out of your groove, and knowing that he is in competition with other guys for your attention is likely to keep him from falling into his groove and pulling you in with him. Not only will you not compromise away the things that are most important to you, you will be exposed to things that you might otherwise never have known existed. And you'll get out of your comfort zone from time to time. Meeting a variety of people will enlarge your world, and help you to see it through another's eyes. Want to be a more well-rounded person? Then date, girl! You'll pursue your own interests, have a diversity of experiences, and never stop learning.

140.

Your dates will reveal their intentions with you faster.

When you are dating several men at the same time, and they know it, each man you go out with is going to do a quick calculation after a few dates about whether or not he wants to keep his hat in the ring. If not, he will soon let you know that he's no longer interested in continuing to date you. And trust me, that is perfectly fine by you. A man who is honest when he loses interest for whatever reasons is free to move on, no harm, no foul. It is when he has lost interest and does not come clean about it that the problems begin. Also, if he is interested, he's going to let you know that too. How will he let you know? He will try harder. He will be more forthcoming with his thoughts and feelings. He will take massive action toward you with the hopes of expansion. Lastly, he will verbalize it. What this means is that dating multiple men takes the guesswork out of dating. No more trying to read his mind and figure it out on your own.

141.

You'll have a basis for comparison when evaluating a guy as a potential partner.

Think about the process of evaluating a potential mate in the same way that you would shop for a car. You want to read *Consumer Reports*, and then take a few things for a test drive, right? Except that there is no consumer report when it comes to picking a mate. You have no choice but to do all of that data gathering yourself. Fortunately there's a way to do that: date multiple men. You don't drive the very first car you see off of the lot. You check out all of them, right? You go to different dealerships. You entertain your *options*. Only then are you likely to end up in a relationship that appeals to both your practical and your sexy sides.

142.

The relationship you do ultimately have will be stronger.

If, after dating multiple men for some time, you do decide to commit to one of them exclusively, you're way ahead of the game. You will already really know each other, and you will have established a level of trust. You will already know how to talk about difficult things, and hopefully will already have let your skeletons out of the closet. You will already know that he values you and treats you well. You will have actual things in common that you like to do, in real time. You will both have dated enough people to really be ready to make a commitment to each other. You will know that the grass is not, in fact, greener, and you will be much less likely to undervalue what you have or to stray. You will also have learned how to be happy without him. You won't *need* him; you will *want* him. He will be the icing on the cake of your life.

143.

Dating multiple guys is the best way to find "the one."

Is there a perfect guy out there for you? Of course there is. Is he perfect? Hell no. But who is? Everyone, no matter how wonderful they are, is going to irritate you from time to time. He will forget things. He will fail. Or maybe he's the type to clam up when something's bothering him, when you really need him to talk it out. Maybe he'll like the same things that you like, or maybe he won't. But what you will find after having dated many, many men over a few years is that the things that fundamentally attract you to a person, the things that you really need in a long-term partner, may not be the things that you thought you did. Whether or not someone is into sports, drinks or doesn't drink, exercises or doesn't exercise, reads or doesn't read is all, essentially, superficial. When you meet the right guy, you will feel it in the very core of your being. There will be something unshakeable between you, and you will recognize its conspicuous presence. You will weigh it against the various gradations of connection that you have felt with other people, and you will "get it." Can you meet this person and have this experience and recognize it for what it is without first dating many men? Sure. You can also win a million dollars in the lottery the first and only time you buy a ticket, but chances are you won't.

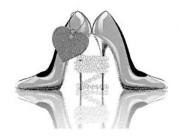

The Dating Diaries

2011 − *Present*

I Deserve a Man Who'll Do Anything to Be My Everything

This week I have had one of the most important revelations to date as a single girl. There was a point in my life that I did not think I deserved the kind of man that would do ANYTHING to be my EVERYTHING. It was not an intentional thought, but I saw myself accepting the man in my life that honestly did NOTHING to be my EVERYTHING. The things he did were things he felt okay with doing or agreed should be done. On the other hand, I found myself doing ANYTHING to be his EVERYTHING. When we first started dating it was funny. For example, we would be going out to dinner and he would ask me what kind of food I was in the mood for. I may say Asian, then he would say he had a taste for Mexican and that there was this Mexican restaurant he wanted to try, and you best believe he would take me to the Mexican restaurant like I had not even said Asian. I know that sounds small, but he was like that with everything, and he thought nothing of it. If I said something about it, he'd say things like, "You know, you should just go with the flow; that's the problem with women, is they don't just go with the flow." It's crazy, because I would *make excuses* for him treating me that way. Ladies, why do we make excuses to stay with a man we know is not good for us? A man that really does not make us feel good from the *inside* out? I was making excuses for him because I did not want to lose him. Then I asked myself, what was I really losing with a man that only did things *he* conveniently wanted to do and *none* of the things that I communicated to him that made me happy? As a single girl, living, learning, laughing, loving and enjoying life to the fullest, *today* I commit to *only* give myself away to a man who will do *anything* to be my *everything*. Why? Because now I realize: I deserve it!

Stop Playing Wife, It Brings Down Your Market Value

Recently I went out to lunch with a guy that I dated ten years ago who honestly was one of the ones that broke my heart. I did everything for this guy. But what I learned after doing "everything" was that he was not "ready." Unfortunately, I did not learn he was not ready until after I had fallen head over heels for him. I cooked; I cleaned; I even would go by the house when he was working late and take out his two dogs—two *big* dogs. I would take his shirts to the cleaners. I even hand washed a pair of his underwear when we were traveling together. You know ladies, we always pack extra everything. But him . . . nope. He packed just enough to get him through our planned trip. Well, the trip was amaze-balls, so we decided to stay. It was absolutely one of the most romantic trips I had ever taken . . . at that point in my life. Since then, there have been lots of trips that blow that one out of the water. That was eleven years ago, so back then we could not afford some of the things that would have enhanced the travel itinerary. Needless to say, none of that mattered. We stayed an extra day and I hand washed his drawers.

The countless breakfasts in bed with French toast croissants, chicken sausage, eggs with spinach, tomatoes and cheese; the crab, shrimp and lobster fettuccine dinners; taking lunch to his job; picnics in the park; taking his mama to her doctors' appointments . . . all of it ran across my mind as I sat at the Commerce Club overlooking Atlanta. He is now a huge real estate developer, not married, no kids. Never engaged. A part of me thought, okay, this may be something. We were smiling at each other in a way that said, "It ain't over. It was just on pause." After lunch we continued the conversation and moved into the lounge area for cocktails. The Commerce Club is a private, members only country club in Atlanta that is connected to all of the other private exclusive clubs. He chose this place for our lunch date to let me know that he is doing well. He wanted to make a statement and he did. I was impressed. He showed me pictures of his seven bedroom, eight bathroom, four-car garage home, complete with an in-law suite. In the picture, the home was surrounded by snow. It was absolutely amazing. I could not stop looking at that picture. I fantasized how it would feel to live in that house, to cook in that kitchen, to sleep in that bed in the master bedroom. Yes, I did. At that moment I was willing to believe that everything I had known him to be ten years ago had changed, that he and I were finally on the same page. He realized that he missed me and wanted me back in his life. We finished lunch and our cocktails in the lounge. He walked me to the elevator, gave me a hug, and patted me on my butt while making a sly comment that he was glad I "still got it." I smiled and said something flirty. He said he wanted to show me his house and that I should come over one day.

I asked him what he missed most about me? He said he always loved how I took care of the home and him. It started going through my head that maybe he was the one. I instantly wanted to start doing all those things that I had done for him before; I wanted to 'play wife' again. He misses me, I thought. He had always been a kind man. We always had a good time together. The fantasy of us together again was enticing for me . . . Wait! No. Stop. Rewind.

The *only* thing he mentioned that he missed was the way I took care of him and his house, I thought to myself. That was my value-added to our relationship that he expressed he missed the most. That's it, I thought? Shucks . . . me 'playing wife' to him and getting lost in him overshadowed everything else that was valuable about me. I am certainly more than cooking and cleaning. We did so much more than that together, too. But that is what he remembered the most. Me playing wife brought down my value. We never talked about the deep stuff. We enjoyed each other, and we never discussed the real partnership or high-market-value questions. The fun, his lifestyle, his success; I got wrapped up into all of it. And a part of me was ready to pick things back up right where we had left off—in his new house.

But I didn't. Instead I looked at him, smiled, and then I got on the elevator and left. I believe that in doing so, my value increased. He is still calling today. Instead of seeing him at his house, we meet out for dinner, or a movie, or whatever—but not at his home. I am not ready for that. And what I am not ready for, I refuse to do. That's that.

Changing *My Mind's* Reality

I received an email this week from a guy asking if all I planned to do with my The Single Girls Club Diaries (TSGCD) blog was "male bash." I looked over the seven TSGCD blog posts and honestly didn't see any of them as "male bashing." My posts are diaries of my honest experiences as a single girl. Any catharsis that I have and then post is a result of those experiences and is very personal to me. If I can't be honest about my own experiences as a single woman, then why do the blog? If my experiences were different, then the point of view would be different.

Feeling like what I'm experiencing as a single woman is *only* happening to me is the worst feeling in the world, and unnecessary, when in reality there are thousands of single ladies going through the same thing. I am growing and learning more about myself, and writing honestly is allowing me to get closer to understanding who I am as a woman, what I want my life to represent, and what I know I deserve. But the comment he made did lead me to examine a way that I could actively change my truth and experiences. I began searching the internet for real life stories/testimonies and videos of guys who were different from the guys I had attracted into my life up till now. My goal was to change my physical reality by first changing my "mind reality."

I could not create the reality to attract a man who would do anything to be my everything, or as my dear friend and relationship coach, Charles Johnson, would call D.I.C.E. (dependable, inspiring, complementary and enhancing)—not with my current "mind reality." As a child, I wasn't raised around men who were D.I.C.E. So what chance did I have to develop a "mind reality" that believed that men outside of the ones I saw growing up even existed?

I started consciously reading stories about men who were different than the types of men I saw as a kid. I started looking at movies that put a spotlight on the "good guy;" men that are D.I.C.E. I believed that by pouring new stories into my psyche about men who were different than what I saw as a child, I would change my "mind's reality;" my belief about what was real and what could exist. Only then would I be able to attract into my life the kind of man that I knew had been purposed for me; the kind of man I knew I deserved; the kind of man that was D.I.C.E. I believe changing my mind's reality has subconsciously created a space in my mind where the reality is that men who are D.I.C.E. do exist. I am now attracting a different kind of man than I ever have before. And it all started from changing the truth in my mind about what a man could and should be.

We're Dating and You're Texting Me Merry Christmas? WTH? Not Acceptable . . . Period

Christmas this year was fantastic! I spent Christmas morning with my baby sister. She cooked a delicious breakfast for me, then we went to see the movie *Selma*. For dinner we went to one of my besties', Dr. Zelda Pittman's, for dinner. Good food, good conversation, good people. After that I went to work to be on air at V-103, 1am-6am. Wooohooo . . . this girl was a busy bee; my schedule was stacked to capacity. Since my mom passed in 2005, I am usually home by myself for Christmas. So hanging out and spending time with my folks was turning a new leaf. The sad moments came and I cried, but then I pushed through. My mom was married five times. She was very passive aggressive. She loved love and her way of keeping it around was suppressing her needs. She catered to the men in her life. What I saw her do impacted my life and the decisions I have made with men. I have struggled to understand my worth and what I need, but—no more struggling.

What I need and what makes me happy has moved to the front of the line in all areas of my life, but especially with men. It did not used to be that way. I used to lie to myself a lot. I would date men that I knew were not good for me; men for whom I would have to suffocate all of who I was to be with them; men to whom I would give 100% without getting their 100% back. For instance, one Christmas, none of the guys I was dating called to wish me a Merry Christmas. They each sent a text. WTH! That was not cool . . . and definitely something that I let them all know is not acceptable. If we are dating—if we are spending time together and I am important to you—sending me a text saying Merry Christmas is not acceptable to me. Back in the day, if something like this had happened, I would not have said anything. I was not very good at explaining my needs and what I wanted. If the guy was not what I needed him to be off the rip, I would delete him out of my phone or put him in my phone as DNA (Do Not Answer). I basically disappeared on them. I did not like confrontation at all. After time, though, I decided that maybe I should be more accommodating. I went from labeling them DNA to just becoming a doormat. You remember the girl barking on one leg in the movie *Coming to America*? That was me. The men would "shhhhh" me, and then I would "shhhh" myself to hold on to them. No more! I am all of me. I am a new Stacii Jae. No more "shhhhhing" me! No more questioning why I want what I want. I go beyond the call of duty, if I am dating a man I like, in order to make him happy. I deserve the same. So texting me for holidays, birthdays, etc. is no longer acceptable. I am not the girl I used to be. I know my worth, and I am courageous enough to let my worth be known. It's not being confrontational, it's me expressing what I need. I am in the business of knowing what makes me happy and letting anyone in my life know it as well. And if you want to be in my life, you will meet the request period point blank. The end.

Ladies, we have to be clear on what we want. Start this next week off asking yourself—what makes you happy? We can't be afraid to make sure the people in our lives know what makes us happy. And not just the men we date, marry, etc. This goes for anyone in our lives. We bend over backwards for the people in our lives, but then let them off easy when it comes to how they treat us. Let's make sure the people in our lives know what we need from them to make us happy. If we don't, no one else will. One thing is for sure; the man you are dating, or your husband, or your kids, etc. have no problem telling you what they need to make them happy, so why the heck should we have a problem doing the same?

Mr. Valentine's Mothballs

It was Valentine's Day. Now, I can honestly say, if I had a choice—if I was any of who I used to be—my Valentine's Day would not have been spent with *him*. Why? First of all, I estimated him to be about twenty years older than me; and second of all, everything in him looked it. I had never been out with him before that night, but I could sense it from the moment that I met him. Mothballs—I could smell the mothballs. Is that wrong? I should not have been thinking of mothballs while we were talking.

The party was fab. It was a doctor's party—doctors were being honored—at this mansion in Buckhead. Buckhead is an area in Atlanta where the who's who live. Mansion . . . well you know what that means: *big ass house*. That's where I met. I'll call him, "Mr. Valentine's Mothballs." He could not stop talking; he had obviously been drinking. Liquor makes some people go on and on and on. Anywho . . . that is what he did. Now . . . there was something cute about him at first; something intriguing. He was funny. He made me laugh, and he had a good energy. There was nothing sleazy about him. I asked him how old he was, and he told me . Yikes! Twenty years older than me . . . Okay. But all I could think was that maybe he could show me things I had not seen. I was so ready to ride a new ride. Do something different. I was tired of the same ole same ole. I longed for new experiences to create new memories. I was open. One of the things I never want to be is eighty years old, sitting in a chair with no memories to pull from, not having lived any real life. What I want is to sit in my chair and have a myriad of absolutely *amazing* memories to pull from—some to make me laugh and some to make me cry. Memories are important. And I thought, as I talked to Mr. Valentine's Mothballs, that he could give me some. Plus, he made me laugh.

Talking to him was different than talking to younger guys. We talked about music. He was from Detroit, the home of Motown. He told me about the Matadors, who eventually changed their name to The Miracles. He spoke about how back in the day you could see The Marvelettes playing at any of the local jam spots. He said he had even known Berry Gordy. The music at the party was amazing.

Physically, he was not my type for many reasons. He was much older than anyone I had ever dated. But I ended up giving him my number anyway. As strange as it sounds, I was kinda drawn to him. He had an innocence about him that was attractive to me. Although, when he laughed, he would push me. Not to hurt me, of course; I know you have met a person that laughed so hard they had to hit something? I had fun with him. We danced. I love to dance. Most guys I had dated didn't like to dance, so when we went out, we never danced. But Mr. Valentines Mothballs was different. He enjoyed dancing. He seemed free. I could tell that he had a certainty to who he was and what he stood for that was different than most younger guys in their late 30's early 40's. We talked music. We shared our journey with each other. He gave me some of the best advice. His stories were interesting to me. With him, I was listening. Soaking it all in. I enjoyed him. I learned from my date with Mr. Valentine's Mothballs. I learned to not judge a book by its cover. My date with him was the best date I had that year. And it's funny, suddenly, he didn't smell like mothballs—no. He smelled like a nice strong cologne and cigars.

You're the Type of Woman That...

Uggghhhhh . . . Coming back home after a bad date is the worst. Why? Because I was actually hoping it would not be. It started off rocky, improved, but went way downhill after that. He was tall, like 6'4", 225 and foine. We went to Houston's. I *love* Houston's. I could eat there every Tuesday and Thursday; those are the two days a week that they have the tortilla soup. Damn, that soup is so good. Anywho . . . he was late. I *hate* late. Why? Because to me, unless it is a family emergency, something at work or car issues, there is no excuse. If I can get through traffic and arrive on time, so can you. But he didn't, so I ended up having a margarita at the bar. I love the bar margaritas at Houston's. They are so yummy. They go kinda overboard on the ice to where if I am drinking the margarita like a limeade or something, it can be gone bye bye rather fast. So, in twenty minutes I had two margaritas and some spinach dip. Now I am thinking, I hope this man is not standing me up. I mean, I have to ask myself that when it's been twenty minutes and he's still not there. I have to ask myself, "Am I going to have to pay this bill for two, going on three, margaritas and spinach dip?" Can you say, *not happy*? I could have been at the crib watching *Scandal* instead of watching it on my DVR later. That's right, I was missing *Scandal* for a date. Who doesn't miss *Scandal* for a date? I know if you were on television and Kerry Washington had a date on the night your show came on, she would DVR it. Get your life. She would. Anywho . . . but look at me now—missing *Scandal* and no man. Geeezzz. Until . . . BAM! In he walks, looking amaze-balls. Well, not really, because I don't know him like that—YET. Just kidding.

Now, this guy and I go out once a month on average, and I do like him. But *really* do I like him? I feel like K. Michelle and that "Love 'Em All" song. I like you when I am around you. And if I am not . . . well, there you have it. I believe when the *right* one comes along, I will be a one-man type girl. I was one for most of my life, but no more. So, until then, let the games begin.

So there he was, standing tall, looking like a piece of milk chocolate Lindt candy being escorted by the hostess to me at the bar. He grabbed me around my waist and cuffed my butt in his hands as he hugged me. I liked it, and decided to forget that I had been waiting for thirty minutes; at least for now. Plus, this guy and I had a thing. For six months we had been on a one-date-a-month plan. That was good for me. He was busy, and so was I. We had not been intimate sexually. This time, though, he sits down and the conversation starts to go in a new direction. When he said, "I can tell you are the type of woman who . . ." I knew we were headed in the wrong direction. As far as I was concerned, he had not spent enough time with me to generalize me as being "the type of woman" that did anything but see him at a restaurant once a month for 6 months. But I let him continue and did not interrupt, because I needed to see *exactly* the type of woman I was—as far as he was concerned, at least.

So he said, "I can tell you are the type of woman that does not know how to take care of her man . . . can't stay in your place and just support him." It went on and on and on. I was like, WTF?!? Because this is a guy that I enjoyed seeing each month for dinner. We had established our date flow, and it was none of this, "who I am as a woman in a relationship," which was none of his business to discuss. He had nothing solid to go on. I let him carry on for a while, and then I asked him how he had concluded that I was that type of woman? He said he could just tell because after our monthly date I did not stay in touch with him to check on him, and I never offered to cook for him. Why would I cook for him? I thought. Why would I do anything but show up and have the wonderful time we had together over dinner, chatting? I was so damn mad. I had waited on this fool for thirty minutes, and then he was going to tell me the type of woman I am NOT.

Finally, after I ordered my Hawaiian steak, kale salad and corn with another margarita, I politely told him in my non-confrontational voice that he was exactly right, I was not that type of woman—to him. I knew it was going to be my last time seeing this idiot, so I also told him why I was not that type of woman to him, and it was real simple: because he is not the type of man that deserves it from me. If he was, then I would be that type of woman. I don't just go around cooking for men and taking care of them. There are levels to a relationship, and he just never hit that level. I told him I actually take very good care of a man that I am dating exclusively. He knew nothing about my French toast banana breakfast croissants, with eggs scrambled in spinach, tomato and cheese, smothered red potatoes, apple smoked bacon or spinach feta chicken sausage.

A Real Woman Can Do It All, But a Real Man Won't Let Her

I have to admit that I have a challenge dating outside of my race. I am just not usually attracted to white men. Recently, though, I did meet someone and we have gone out on occasion. This man is *never* late. If he says 5:30 p.m., he is at my condo by no later than 5:20 p.m. I feel bad because I am never ready, but he never complains. He says he may smoke weed on occasion. What does that have to do with anything? Well, everything. I do not know many white dudes that smoke weed, so for me it gives him some swag and makes him a bit more interesting. Sad, but true . . . LOL. Anywho, I have been enjoying him. I know it's in my head, but I think people are staring at us when we are out. It could be because usually when I see an interracial couple and I am out, I do give them an extra stare.

He is absolutely one of the most helpful guys I am dating. Moving has been so stressful, and also very frustrating, because none of the guys I am dating, outside of this one, has offered to help me move. I like him, but I wonder why none of the other men in my life, whom I also like, have offered to help me. I am a girl; I have soft and silky skin; girl curves and long hair;

I love frilly things, glitter, stilettos; and I have standing facial and mani/pedi appointments. I love getting my makeup done, and I love getting flowers. Point blank—I am girl times ten trillion. Everything about me is woman. *Nothing* about me screams that I'm a dude and like doing dude stuff like moving heavy boxes, rolling dollies or any other male testosterone type moving duties. But for some reason, no matter how girlie I am, *none* of my male suitors helped, or even called and inquired if I needed help. Well, none of the black guys I am dating did. Hurtful, honestly. But was this my fault? And if so, I was not sure what I had done to give them the impression that I didn't need help. Because baaaabbbyyyy . . . I am *quite* the opposite. I need help and would gladly welcome it, if offered. The more I thought about it, I wondered, did they think that because I take care of myself so well that I did not need their help? I was pretty happy with the other guys that I'd been dating and really did not want to walk away from either of them. They are fun and the conversation I had with each of them was stimulating. But after the move and absolutely no help from any of them, outside of my Caucasian male suitor, I started to feel some kind of way about all of them. I no longer enjoyed the conversations or the dates.

Finally I asked them about it, and this is what I was told:

Reason 1: I did not ask for help.

Reason 2: He did not want to look like he was intruding on my personal space.

Reason 3: He did not think I needed help.

Men need to understand, when they see a single woman like me and my fellow sister girls out there in singlehood who are also doing it *all*—taking care of our lives well— it's because we have to do it all by ourselves, not because we want to.

After spending some time contemplating whether or not I had done something to make a man think I want to do things like pick up boxes and move dollies alone without any help, and listening to the answers from the guys I was dating, I came to the conclusion that a *real man* would know that a *real woman* can do it all by herself, but a *real man* would not let her. As I completed my move out of my old condo and into my new one, I realized that I did not have any real men in my life. So I decided, out with the old place and old guys and in with the new—all new *everything*!

Mr. Half

Have you ever known the dude that no matter what you asked him for, he would always only give you half? I mean, it doesn't make a difference what it was or how much it was . . . he was *always* only willing to give you *half*. What is that about? I cannot understand the logic in Mr. Half. Is it something that their fathers told them? If she asks for $50 son, you should never give her more than $25? I am still trying to understand the reasoning behind that thought process. I know I am not supposed to count nobody's money, but if I need help and we are dating exclusively and you have it, shouldn't the mission, the objective, and the goal be to give me ALL of what I ask for? If somebody asks me for $50 and I have $50 to give, then dammit I am going to give them $50. Period point blank. Am I supposed to just be happy with what I am given? Should I not say, "Mr. Half, what's up with your thought process, honey?"

I guess that would be rude, asking why half all the time. But why is that rude? In my opinion, it's rude to not give me what I ask for if we are dating and you have it. And honestly it could be me, because not one man has done this but several. Mr. Half gives me half and expects "wholes" from me. Nah, son. No wholes here. We do half for half. I was raised to do unto others as they do unto you. So please, Mr. Half, do not call me asking me for something and think you are going to get whole.

I was talking to a group of single ladies about living a full life: living, laughing, learning, loving in the fullness of who they are. And honestly, I had to pull my coat tail. I attracted men who believed in living their life choices with me in half because in mind, body and spirit I was only half. I would like to tell people differently, but tucked in the pages of my diary, I have to be honest with at least myself and say that my half back in the day attracted another half. No way could he give me anything whole when he was half of the man who he was born to be and I was half of the woman I was born to be. For my part, I realized that my power lies in me accepting responsibility for attracting the things that I have I attracted into my life. Including the men I had attracted. I started looking at my "self-talk," and I realized that self-talk created a bubble around me that was at the head of what I was attracting in my life. I could no longer blame or question the men around me, because they were a reflection of me. I had to do the work on me to become whole.

The work? Well that is a much longer story than Mr. Half. Full of complexity. But after I started doing the work on myself—turning the finger back around at myself instead of out at someone else—and asking myself the hard questions about who I was and why I was here, I saw the difference in me. Other people saw it, too. I started meeting men who wanted to settle down. I started to attract whole men, who wanted to give me all of themselves. I started attracting men who wanted to give me their whole. No more half men came my way because there was no more half me. I had to ask myself, was I really ready to give up the whole of myself? And honestly, the answer is no. Not unless it is right. Until then, I am selfish with my whole—unapologetically. My grandmother says, "But the clock is ticking, baby." I still say, "Moment to moment. The only time is the present time."

Finding Peace through the Process

A big day tomorrow for me. I'm so excited. I have a big audition with the casting director I've been trying to get to see me forever. I'm ready, too. This is my time. Outside of booking the gig, I wanna show myself that I can do this; that I am good at this acting thing. It's been a long time since my old movies, *Thin Line Between Love and Hate* (Peaches) and *How To Be a Player* (Sherri). I hate to audition. But it's part of the process. To win, I have to go through it.

Same thing with my losing weight. It's coming off slowly. But it is coming off. I have to keep doing what I am doing to keep the weight coming off, even if it's just a little bit at a time.

Process.

It's the same thing as succeeding as a radio personality. I was sharing with someone about how I had been given the opportunity to do some things as a personality that I had not been given before, and they said something that really spoke to me. They said, "See? It's baby steps. But it's still steps. It's all part of the process." I'm learning that everything is process.

Which brings me to this: my singlehood. Tonight I am having dinner alone at the local bar across the street from my condo. It's me and my iPad. Looking around at the tables full with couples out chatting it up, I said to myself, "Where is my boyfriend?" But then I thought, is that what I really want? I would have had to make different choices today and be concerned with someone else and their needs. No matter if he would have given me my space; there would have still been a level of concern for him because that's just who I am. But I have to be honest; as it is, I can go back home after I leave here to the same peaceful quiet space that I left, and have a glass of wine, look at a movie, write, read or do whatever I want to do. Period point blank.

So, am I really ready for a relationship? Is what I feel right now something that people in relationships feel? I am sure of it. I have spoken to girlfriends before who have mentioned that they wish they had more time for themselves away from the kids and the man. Some of them take the time away. But I honestly don't think that the need for "time away" is what I feel right now. No way it can be.

There is a sort of freedom and peace that I feel in singlehood that only singlehood can bring. And right now, at this moment in time, I'm happy that I'm single. 100%. I believe that right now so many things in my life are in the process phase that having a kid, relationship or marriage would just interrupt the processes. I am in the process of discovering and realizing who I am; my power as a human being, and as a woman. I am in the process of discovering what my contribution to this world will be.

I'm in process.

It's better for me to go through this process and have clarity about those things before I am one with someone else. I believe that once I complete the process and have the answers I need then he—what my girl Nina Brown calls #theonlyexception—will come. And honestly, no matter what I say on those days when I say that I want him now, I don't. I really want him when I am through being processed.

Mr. Short Stop

Well, I can honestly say I didn't used to date a guy that is 5'4". All I could think sitting across from him was how very short boys grow up to be very short men. And I want to have *no* part of that. It is the same with short teeth. You know how sometimes men have baby teeth, meaning all of them, and they are *all* gums? I was not having anything short. But recently, after doing some soul searching, I decided to open my mind up and explore other territories. I met Mr. Short Stop at the 2014 Who's Who in Black Atlanta unveiling. I was the publisher for the 15th edition, and Mr. Short Stop was one of the executives we honored in that edition. I honestly had no idea who he was before reading his submission. But on paper he was extremely impressive. He was attractive, and initially I could not tell how tall he was.

On the evening of the event, I saw him from a distance and was shocked that he was a little man. No more than 5'6". I am 5'4", so that night with heels on I was much, much taller than him. I stand about 5'9" with heels on. Needless to say, he congratulated me on the event, which was definitely a success. We ended up doubling the sales from previous years and attendance for the unveiling was sold out. There were more than a thousand people in attendance. He was very handsome, but he was just much shorter than I liked. I never really dated a guy that was not at least 5'10". Anything shorter was just unacceptable. Any time a short man had approached me in the past, I could not get past looking at him and thinking that my sons would be short, and most women—including, probably, his mom—like tall men. I would also think that my son would be like, "Mom, what the hell? You knew this man was short and look what you did to me!" I am only kidding, maybe it would not be that extreme. But I did often think, when approached by a short man for a date, about my unborn sons. It would be okay if the girl was short. I am short.

But Mr. Short Stop was different. He stood tall. It was not just his success, either. I had been approached by a successful short man in the past, but it was too much of a risk. His arms were short too. I saw that he could gain weight more quickly as he aged, and then he would be a short and fat old man. But this time I was in a different place. I was not looking at every date as a potential husband. I just wanted to date and have a good time. Kids and all the rest meant nothing to me at this point. I was committed to taking each date one day at a time. So I met him out at The Lobster Bar in Buckhead. I had a ribeye steak and he had the Chilean sea bass. I love a ribeye steak. We had appetizers, and he made me laugh hysterically. He actually made a joke and said that he never thought I would say yes, that I come off as one of those girls who only dates tall guys. I was reluctant at first to answer, but I told him he was right. We laughed and continued to enjoy the evening.

He wasn't put off or upset with my honesty at all, which totally impressed me.

As he walked me to the car that night after dinner, he asked me for another date. I have to be honest, I enjoyed him. Yes he was very short; much shorter than I was attracted to; but I had had fun, so I accepted. We went out again the following week, and I had a great time. I can say that much of our dates are filled with laughter. He has the funniest stories of growing up, and some of the shenanigans he gets to do with his work colleagues are crazy. He travels a lot, so our dates are sporadic, but I can say that Mr. Short Stop is still in my life today. I continue to get to know him and date him when he is in town, and he is at least 5'10" to me now. I am happy that I allowed myself to get past my initial hang ups about his height. I do not know if we will ever be more than what we are today, but allowing myself to open my mind and date outside of the parameters I originally set for myself has been a much better way of dating.

I Heard a Girl Should Be Like a Butterfly...Can I Be Like a Butterfly and Still Twerk On Occasion?

Recently I read this post that said, "A girl should be like a butterfly. Pretty to *see*, hard to *catch*." I totally believe this. But I have one question . . . Can I hustle, work hard, be committed to making my dreams come true, have a shot or two of my favorite alcoholic beverage, curse on occasion when the situation calls for it and *still* be a butterfly? Can I greet my BFF by calling her the urban name for a "female dog," and also be a top fundraiser for political figures like presidents and mayors, and be of service to the community, but still listen to Nicki Minaj and have a fab fav new song off her new album *The Pinkprint* called "I'm Feeling Myself"? Can I be particularly fond of the song "Anaconda"? Can I be honest and say that right now in my life that I am happy being single, and like K. Michelle I just wanna "Love Em' All?" Can I enjoy watching the antics on reality shows like "The Real Housewives of Atlanta," and "Love & Hip Hop ATL" and be a butterfly? Out of all the quotes from Maya Angelou, I am particularly drawn to the one that says, "I love to see a young girl go out and grab the world by the lapels. Life's a bitch. You've got to go out and kick ass." Maya Angelou was a *butterfly*. So can I be one too, and still speak my mind? Can I have as my favorite books *The Game of Life and How to Play It* by Florence Scovell Shin, *The Purpose Driven Life* by Rick Warren and *The Alchemist* by Paublo Coelho, but still love reading books like *Men Love Bitches* by Sherry Argov and *Confessions of a Video Vixen* by Karrine Stephans? Can I not hold back, and be unapologetic for having an opinion whether you like it or not, walk in a room like I own it and really believe I do, be kind to people but be real clear with you if you are on my "DF witcha' list," be honest with dudes and let them know I only date *one* when *one* shows up, and I know that he is #theonlyexception and is my D.I.C.E. (Dependable, Inspiring, Complementary and Enhancing), believe God and have faith in Him that surpasses understanding, but still like to dance on tables and bars if I want to have that kinda good time, and also *twerk on occasion, and still be a butterfly?* I'm just saying . . . Cuz that's ME!

Fixing Me Is About Me, Not About Me Getting a Man

Recently, I was honored as one of the Top 25 Women in Atlanta by *Rolling Out* magazine. It was an amazing feeling to be celebrated amongst some of the most amazing women in Atlanta. I will never forget that evening. Some of my closest friends attended, as well as Atlanta's Mayor, Kasim Reed, who spoke at the event, and who expressed how happy he was for me to receive such a prestigious honor. It's funny; my journey has been so full of opportunities to express myself in so many different ways, from acting to politics to radio . . . and I am not done. I truly believe there is so much more for me to do, and I plan to do it all. I have not even scratched the surface of the things I plan to accomplish.

I also spoke at the Women's Empowerment Network (WEN) conference where I launched "The Single Girls Club." It was an amazing experience. I wish I had caught it on tape. Stacii Jae's The Single Girls Club Presents: "My Journey to Living, Laughing, Learning, Loving: Changing My Mind's Reality." I led a panel of four dynamic women (married and single): Jamie Foster Brown (Founder and Publisher of Sister 2 Sister Magazine) Monyetta Shaw (VH1, Atlanta Exes),

Dr. Heavenly Kimes (Bravo's Married 2 Medicine) and Marsha Shackelford (Co-Owner, The Buckhead Bottle Bar & Bistro). We were all very honest about our struggles and challenges as single women. I shared a lot about myself and my journey. One thing I did share was that I am not single because there is a shortage of men. I am on a journey to be whole by myself and to be okay with sharing who I am with the world as I tarry along.

To my surprise, the more I shared, the more some of the women in the audience wanted to fix me for the sake of getting a man. Some women started standing up and praying for me. Now, let me say this. My challenges are no deeper than any other woman's challenges, but for the mere fact that I am open about mine and I happen to be single, some of the married women wanted to give me their advice from the standpoint of "fixing" me to get a man. My interest in self-improvement has absolutely nothing to do with a man, and everything to do with me. It's crazy to me that most of the women in the room looked at getting a man as being a kind of reward—all a girl could ever want—6'3", 235 pounds, chocolate and a very good dresser, balanced in all areas . . . foine. I could have it all— and he was all there was; an interesting conversation to be in at a women's empowerment conference. I was sitting there thinking to myself that there are plenty of "broken" women who are married; if all I wanted was a man, I could get married and would not have to "fix" anything about myself. For a second, I thought the "fix it for a man" advice crew was about to come bow their heads, lay hands on me and begin praying.

Jamie Foster Brown shared stories about her father, who constantly told her how special and deserving she was; stories that she will never forget; stories that—at sixty-seven years of age and after forty-five years of marriage to one man—she still carries with her to share with other girls. My reality was different. My father was not around me as I grew up. My ideas and my realities surrounding relationships came from what I saw as a child looking at the relationships that my mom and my grandmother had with men. Both were married multiple times. I also learned from the school of hard knocks. I embrace it though; all fit. It's made me who I am. The single girl I am now is electric! I can be a bit crazy sometimes, and I don't care. I am who I am.

At this WEN conference, as the "fix it for a man" advice crew launched their campaign, I did not back down. I owned who I was, who I am and who I want to be; the things I saw as a child that molded me (good and bad); and my full journey and growth as a single woman. I shared with them that who I want to become, as surprising as this may sound, is the best me I can be, for me. Everything else follows that. The learn aspect of The Single Girls Club mantra is about single women being on a journey with other single women in a safe environment where they don't feel judged, and where they can really talk through their most intimate personal moments, hopefully learning from other single women, as well as bringing in professionals who can help guide them in their journeys and nurture them as well.

I am so excited to have more conversations with single ladies just like we did at WEN. I am equally excited about creating fun events that support the other three aspects of The Single Girls Club mantra. . It's going to be fun!

About the Single Girls Club

The Single Girls Club USA (TSGC) is a community of single women who have formed a support system within various stages of their life journey to connect, build friendships, grow professionally and entrepreneurially, and experience life on their terms.

The mission of TSGC is to provide single females with the tools needed to live a full, whole life. Through an online community and lifestyle event experiences, TSGC is a movement in the tune of "All Things Single," and aims to connect, educate, inspire and empower single women to enjoy their lives to the fullest. Says founder, Stacii Jae, "Our Living, Laughing, Learning, Loving ME! mantra powers us forward in everything we do."

The TSGC Conference is a two-day event full of networking opportunities with dynamic female powerhouses (and some men) sharing life-changing, educational, empowering and confidence-building tools. The TSGC Conference consists of workshops thar empower single women to have healthy relationships, make more money, start businesses and live fuller lives. The full Single Girls Club experience is composed of three events held across the country in various cities: the Single Girls Club Conference, "So Yummy" Single Girls Who Brunch, and Power Dating.

Stacii Jae leads call sessions with single ladies from all over the country called Single Girls Talk, in which she and a male guest celebrity co-host discuss topics that inspire confidence, and give today's single females both the clarity and the power to achieve their fullest personal and professional potential.

For more information about the Single Girls Club, please visit thesinglegirlsclub.com.

About the Author

Stacii Jae Johnson, actress, radio personality, television host, lifestyle influencer and women's empowerment advocate, is vastly becoming the "go-to" for all things single girl. As a former on-air jock at the country's #1 urban radio station, CBS Radio, WVEE-FM V-103, Stacii Jae is a diehard entrepreneur focused on building a media empire. Prior to her arrival at V-103, Stacii Jae created and hosted Atlanta's #1 girl talk radio show, "Black Girls Radio." Originally from Memphis, TN, Ms. Johnson moved to Atlanta to attend the esteemed Spelman College, and then graduated with honors. She is a girl on the move, from Memphis to Atlanta to Hollywood actress and back to Atlanta as a high profile political figure, working in the Office of Atlanta Mayor Kasim Reed as the former Entertainment & Special Events Director, top advisor and a member of his executive leadership team for over three years.

Johnson is a young, vivacious influencer who has had a career of ups and downs. However, when given lemons, Stacii Jae is known to make her famous lemonade. A southern belle at heart, Johnson is a sought after influencer who has lots of irons in the fire. As many can see with her new radio career, Johnson is not afraid of new challenges. She is the founder of The Single Girls Club (TSGC) and writes a monthly blog called The Single Girls Club Diaries. The mission of TSGC is to provide single females with the tools needed to live a full, whole life. Through an online community and lifestyle event experiences, TSGC is a movement in the tune of "All Things Single," and aims to connect, educate, inspire and empower single ladies.

Stacii Jae calls herself the "Multi Dating Philosofixer" - A lover of helping single women fix their dating life by coaching them and guiding their philosophy on how to successfully date multiple people simultaneously. The premise of the Multi Dating Philosofixer is to (1) get single women to stop concentrating on an expected 'result' (2) be open to the journey that each individual date takes them on (3) not hand over monogamy on a silver platter until it is deserving.

TSGC signature events are: The Single Girls Club Conference, Power Dating, Single Girls Talk and Single Girls Who Brunch. "Our Living, Learning, Laughing, Loving ME! mantra powers us forward in everything we do", says Stacii Jae. With a guest celebrity co-host, Stacii Jae leads a weekly call session with single ladies from all over the country called "Single Girls Talk," discussing topics that inspire confidence and give today's single females clarity and power to achieve their fullest personal and professional potential.

As a Hollywood actress, Stacii Jae landed roles in popular productions by You Go Boy! Productions (Martin), Savoy Pictures (How To Be A Player as Sherri) and New Line Cinema (A Thin Line Between Love & Hate as Peaches) as well as television roles on NBC and FOX Networks. Most recently, she was cast in a docu-series premiering this fall called From the

Bottom Up (airing on Centric, Executive Producer, Queen Latifah) about six ladies on the comeback. Stacii is also co-host, with R&B Diva Nicci Gilbert, of Divas & Cocktails, a "no conversation is off-limits" late night talk show covering everything from lifestyle, fashion and celebrity headlines to celebrity dish. Johnson was recently named one of the top 25 women in Atlanta by Steed Media Group, and has earned honors as an "Obama Victory Trustee" and Associate Publisher, Who's Who in Black Atlanta (15th Edition, 2014). Truly in the midst of a chameleon career, Stacii Jae is colorful, bright and true.

For more information about Stacii Jae Johnson, please visit staciijaejohnson.com

If you would like to bring Stacii Jae Johnson to your live event, or book an event with Stacii Jae Johnson, email: BookStaciiJae@staciijaejohnson.com